Figuring Lacan:
Criticism and the Cultural
Unconscious

CRITICS OF THE TWENTIETH CENTURY
Edited by Christopher Norris, University of Wales Institute of
Science and Technology

Titles in preparation:

A. J. Greimas and the Discourses of the Human Sciences
Ronald Schleifer
Raymond Williams
John Higgins
Paul de Man
Richard Machin

Figuring Lacan

Criticism and the Cultural
Unconscious

Juliet Flower MacCannell

UNIVERSITY OF NEBRASKA PRESS
Lincoln

© 1986 Juliet Flower MacCannell

Library of Congress Cataloging-in-Publication Data

MacCannell, Juliet Flower, 1943-
 Figuring Lacan.

 (Critics of the twentieth century)
 Bibliography: p.
 1. Psychoanalysis and literature. 2. Criticism.
3. Lacan, Jacques, 1901- — Contributions in
criticism. I. Title. II. Series.
PN98.P75M3 1986   801'.92   86-11217
ISBN 0-8032-3109-1
ISBN 0-8032-8140-4 (pbk.)

Published in Great Britain and Australia by Croom Helm, Ltd
Published simultaneously in the United States by
the University of Nebraska Press

Printed and bound in Great Britain

Contents

This notion of discourse is to be taken as a social link
founded on language . . .
(Lacan, 'À Jakobson', *XX*, 27)

Editor's Foreword

The twentieth century has produced a remarkable number of gifted and innovative literary critics. Indeed it could be argued that some of the finest literary minds of the age have turned to criticism as the medium best adapted to their complex and speculative range of interests. This has sometimes given rise to regret among those who insist on a clear demarcation between 'creative' (primary) writing on the one hand, and 'critical' (secondary) texts on the other. Yet this distinction is far from self-evident. It is coming under strain at the moment as novelists and poets grow increasingly aware of the conventions that govern their writing and the challenge of consciously exploiting and subverting those conventions. And the critics for their part — some of them at least — are beginning to question their traditional role as humble servants of the literary text with no further claim upon the reader's interest or attention. Quite simply, there are texts of literary criticism and theory that, for various reasons — stylistic complexity, historical influence, range of intellectual command — cannot be counted a mere appendage to those other, 'primary' texts.

Of course, there is a logical puzzle here, since (it will be argued) 'literary criticism' would never have come into being, and could hardly exist as such, were it not for the body of creative writings that provide its *raison d'être*. But this is not quite the kind of knock-down argument that it might appear at first glance. For one thing, it conflates some very different orders of priority, assuming that literature always comes first (in the sense that Greek tragedy had to exist before Aristotle could formulate its rules), so that literary texts are for that very reason possessed of superior value. And this argument would seem to find commonsense support in the difficulty of thinking what 'literary criticism' could *be* if it seriously renounced all sense of the distinction between literary and critical texts. Would it not then find itself in the unfortunate position of a discipline that had willed its own demise by declaring its subject non-existent?

But these objections would only hit their mark if there were indeed a special kind of writing called 'literature' whose difference from other kinds of writing was enough to put criticism firmly in its place. Otherwise there is nothing in the least self-defeating or paradoxical about a discourse, nominally that of literary criticism, that accrues such interest on its own account as to force some fairly drastic rethinking of its proper powers and limits. The act of crossing over from commentary to literature — or of simply denying the difference between them — becomes quite explicit in the writing of a critic like Geoffrey Hartman. But the signs are already there in such classics as William Empson's *Seven Types Of Ambiguity* (1928), a text whose transformative influence on our habits of reading must surely be ranked with the great creative moments of literary modernism. Only on the most dogmatic view of the difference between 'literature' and 'criticism' could a work like *Seven Types* be counted generically an inferior, sub-literary species of production. And the same can be said for many of the critics whose writings and influence this series sets out to explore.

Some, like Empson, are conspicuous individuals who belong to no particular school or larger movement. Others, like the Russian Formalists, were part of a communal enterprise and are therefore best understood as representative figures in a complex and evolving dialogue. Then again there are cases of collective identity (like the so-called 'Yale deconstructors') where a mythical group image is invented for largely polemical purposes. (The volumes in this series on de Man, Hartman, and Bloom should help to dispel the idea that 'Yale deconstruction' is anything more than a handy device for collapsing differences and avoiding serious debate.) So there is no question of a series format or house-style that would seek to reduce these differences to a blandly homogeneous treatment. One consequence of recent critical theory is the realisation that literary texts have no self-sufficient or autonomous meaning, no existence apart from their after-life of changing interpretations and values. And the same applies to those *critical* texts whose meaning and significance are subject to constant shifts and realignments of interest. This is not to say that trends in criticism are just a matter of intellectual fashion or the merry-go-round of rising and falling reputations. But it is important to grasp how complex are the forces — the conjunctions of historical and cultural motive — that affect the first reception and the subsequent fortunes of a critical text. This point has been raised into a systematic programme by critics like Hans-Robert Jauss, practitioners of so-called 'reception theory' as a form of historical hermeneutics. The volumes in this series will therefore be concerned not only to expound what is of lasting significance but also to set these critics in the context of present-day argument and debate. In some cases (as with Walter Benjamin) this debate takes the form of a struggle for inter-pretative power among disciplines with sharply opposed ideo-logical viewpoints. Such controversies cannot simply be ignored in the interests of achieving a clear and balanced account. They point to unresolved tensions and problems which are there in the critic's work as well as in the rival appropriative readings. In the end there is no way of drawing a neat methodological line between 'intrinsic' questions (what the critic really thought) and those other, supposedly 'extrinsic' concerns that have to do with influence and reception history.

The volumes will vary accordingly in their focus and range of coverage. They will also reflect the ways in which a speculative approach to questions of literary theory has proved to have striking consequences for the human sciences at large. This breaking-down of disciplinary bounds is among the most signifi-cant developments in recent critical thinking. As philosophers and historians, among others, come to recognise the rhetorical complexity of the texts they deal with, so literary theory takes on a new dimension of interest and relevance. It is scarcely appro-riate to think of writers like Derrida or de Man as literary critics in any conventional sense of the term. For one thing, they are as much concerned with 'philosophical' as with 'literary' texts, and have indeed — both of them — actively sought to subvert (or deconstruct) such tidy distinctions. A principal object in planning this series was to take full stock of these shifts in the wider intellectual terrain (including the frequent boundary disputes) brought about by critical theory. And, of course, such changes are by no means confined to literary studies, philosophy and the so-called 'sciences of man'. It is equally the case in (say) nuclear physics and molecular biology that advances in the one field have decisive implications for the other, so that specialised research often tends (paradoxically) to break down existing divisions of knowledge. Such work is typically many years ahead of the academic disciplines and teaching institutions that have obvious reasons of their own for preserving the intellectual *status quo*. One important aspect of modern critical theory is the challenge it presents to these traditional ideas. And lest it be thought that this is merely a one-sided takeover bid by the literary critics, the series will include a number of volumes by authors in those other disciplines, including, for instance, a study of Roland Barthes by an American analytical philosopher.

We shall not, however, cleave to theory as a matter of polemical or principled stance. The series will extend to figures like F. R. Leavis, whose widespread influence went along with an express aversion to literary theory; scholars like Erich Auerbach in the mainstream European tradition; and others who resist assimilation to any clear-cut line of descent. There will also be authoritative volumes on critics such as Northrop Frye and Lionel Trilling, figures who, for various reasons, occupy an ambivalent or essentially contested place in modern critical tradition. Above all the series will strive to resist that current polarisation of attitudes that sees no common ground of interest between 'literary criticism' and 'critical theory'.

CHRISTOPHER NORRIS

Acknowledgements

A variety of persons and events in my life worked together to inspire this book. I have been for several years writing a manuscript on love and desire in eighteenth- and nineteenth-century authors — principally Rousseau and Stendhal — and have often been guided in my research by Lacan's writing. It became increasingly apparent to me that much of what I was doing would be fruitless if I did not make clear relatively quickly how the structure of Lacan's thought both continues and renews the understanding of desire which I found in my early authors. In 1983 I received a Faculty Fellowship from the Academic Senate of the University of California, Irvine, to carry on this bi-directional study, mainly on Stendhal and Lacan. Without this generous grant, and a subsequent Summer Fellowship from Dean Kendall Bailes of the School of Humanities at UCI, this work would not have been possible. Later, in 1983, I was invited to contribute to a special issue of *Modern Language Notes* on Lacan and narration edited by Robert Con Davis. I wish to thank Professors Leonard Tennenhouse and Nancy Armstrong who first suggested to me the possibility of doing a book on Lacan and who brought my work to the attention of Christopher Norris, general editor of the *Critics of the Twentieth Century* series. His encouragement has been most helpful.

My students in the course on 'Desire in Literature' at UCI were inspirational in their reception of some of the readings in this book.

I owe a debt of gratitude for the teaching of the late Paul de Man, who was my mentor and adviser, and whose approach to the figurative word was remarkably close to Lacan's.

My warmest thanks I reserve for my husband, Dean MacCannell, and my sons, Daniel and Jason, whose approach to the witty word is remarkably close to Lacan's.

Preface

*There is no doubt that it is madness for a man to lay himself open to
passionate love. Sometimes, however, the cure acts too drastically.
Young American girls in the United States are so imbued and fortified
with rational ideas that love, the flower of life, has deserted their youth.
In Boston a girl can quite safely be left alone with a handsome
stranger, in the certainty that she will think of nothing but the income
of her future husband.*

(Stendhal, No. 40 'Various fragments' *Love*,[1] 225)

Reading through Lacan, the *Ecrits*, but especially the seminars
published in *Ornicar?* and *Scilicet*, one finds oneself inevitably
in the position of the student. It is an enviable position, one we
are not often able to re-enter so easily as with this obscure stylist,
this circuitous lecturer: with Lacan we can simply read, without
the compulsion to write, to work it all out, to know. We are
never held responsible, by Lacan, for absolute knowledge.

His discourse is set towards undermining discourse as a programme leading towards knowledge, and it might seem to
favour and privilege the student who would remain an 'imbe-
cile'. After all, 'imbecility', Lacan writes, 'is that by which the
body attests to being alive' (*Ornicar?* 1975, 91, Sem. 10,
December 1974). Language delivers us not to life but to death, at
least symbolically, it replaces the body: ' "Life" for language is
other than what one calls life. Drives which elevate this life to
language make as much of a place for that which, in terms of
somatic support, signifies death' (*Ornicar?* 11, 1977, 5).
Shakespeare knew that the discourse of a Fool is, in confusing
times, wiser than that of the Sage. Should we not prefer life to
death? In short, why subject ourselves to language, or to
language as symbolic?

But if to be intelligent is to read 'through' someone, or as
Lacan points to the etymology of intelligence — *inter-legere*, to
read between the lines — then this, Lacan continues, is to 'know
otherwise than the manner in which the symbolic is written' (91).
Lacan is effacing the simple opposition of mind and body,
knowledge and ignorance, life and death. And he insists on

doing so through a certain kind of *reading*.

Lacan characterised his own enterprise as 'commenting' on the texts of Freud, a layering of another text over his. The two form an allegorical relationship in Walter Benjamin's sense of the term. If we read Freud 'through' (in the sense of via, by means of) Lacan we can also reverse the process. Such a reading is aimed at bringing certain things to centre-stage, things that remain occulted or hidden by the lucidity of the one, the obscurity of the other.

I have found it helpful in undertaking the task I set of 'figuring' Lacan by reading through him (in both senses of the term) to keep Freud's text in view, his general enterprise, his starting-points, his aims. At the same time, I have tried to avoid the common pitfall, in figuring Lacan, of substituting Freud for him. The two discourses differ substantially, and their differences are significant for what I am attempting here, which is to give some sense of Lacan's *criticism*.

For if the critical side of Freud's discourse has become blunted by familiarity, by partial adoptions, by misprision, it is Lacan's lot to renew the critical spirit of that enterprise. Using boldly the techniques of defamiliarisation taught by formalism, Lacan reverses some of Freud's priorities, taking off from a different starting-point (although not with a different aim) to criticise human culture and its misadventures.

Freud, assuming the position of the Victorian man, centres his analysis on individual actors in order to implicate — and indict — their minutest acts in a vast cultural process of restrictions and negations that can be read through any failures that occur in the course of performing these acts. Taking that which everyone took for granted — civilised behaviour, the normal person — Freud estranged these concepts and showed their positioning by a general imperative to sacrifice immediacy and pleasure for future 'enjoyment', to the profit of a culture whose sole aim was to perpetuate, to reproduce itself.

Lacan, situated in a mass culture which has largely taken the problem of reproducing itself out of the hands of individuals altogether, employing almost unimaginable technologies to this end, no longer takes 'people' as his norm. Things have gone well beyond that. So much so that Lacan rarely uses the example of any individual performance, any face-to-face interaction, any particular everyday *lapsus* as a subject for his analysis. Beginning instead with an opposing assumption to that of Freud, one that makes of the symbolic order the overt, the immediate, rather than the ultimate context of human life, Lacan focuses his impressive analytic powers on symbols, metaphors, words. They motivate human behaviour; they *are* human behaviour. 'Some people,' he writes, 'feel the weight of words' (*Scilicet* 6/7, 1976, 46).

For Lacan, the human being lives in a new order ('un ordre nouveau'), (*I*, xix, 263)[2] created by the symbol; more specifically, and 'at the letter', the word. He calls it a new 'dit-mention' (*Ornicar?* 11, 1977, 4) presided over by a 'd-i-t' (*déité* or god, as well as the present tense and past participle of 'to say'). You have to understand the multiple significances of words, but more importantly, you have to understand their uses. His emphasis is not, as it is in Freud, on where the person falls, slips, fails to uphold the imperatives of civilisation. It is on the places where persons adhere all too fully to the demands of the Symbolic Order, where what fails is *resistance* to its demands, not adherence or obedience to them.

A different angle, then, but in the spirit of Freud. Lacan never centres his own analyses on the mutual co-presence of two human beings — this perhaps in the spirit also of Engels and his critique of Dühring's mythical 'two persons' who are supposed to have founded society — because such a situation has never really existed. For Lacan, culture (and I am deliberately avoiding recourse to the more restricted term 'language' even though it is in more current use, because it is culture and its imperatives that Lacan's criticism concerns) pulls us all together and makes us specifically 'human beings'. But to do so, it must also keep us apart within this human sphere. Culture sustains human intercourse — by preventing it.

'Reading through Lacan', then, is not perhaps as carefree an undertaking as I suggested at the outset. In reading through Lacan we shall always make a tie to him. It is the *way* in which this link will be made that worries Lacan. For Lacan, discourse is what 'determines the form of a social tie' (Mitchell, 153).[3] The discourse of the teacher and the social tie formed with the student is only one among the several Lacan explicates. But in so far as the student–teacher link is one of the forms by which culture is reproduced, Lacanian pedagogy is implicated in his general cultural critique.

It is not easy to leave the path that runs between the silences of imbecility and knowledge: the student may get called on. Consider now the following vignette from a student–professor relationship in Lacan. In his remarks prefacing Anika Lemaire's (1970) study,[4] Lacan appears to be somewhat pleased by the recent attention to his writings, which included Anthony Wilden's *Language of the Self*, as well as Lemaire's study, with a preface by Antoine Vergote. Lacan comments in passing on the appropriateness of the initial of each commentator's forename being the capital letter A ('Anthony, Anika . . . what sign of a new wind is insisting in these initials?', p. vii). He also, characteristically, chides the enterprise: Lacan presents himself as sceptical of the fact that his articles are being subjected to academic analytical discourse:

> My *Ecrits* are unsuitable for a thesis, particularly an academic thesis: they are antithetical by nature: one either takes what they formulate or one leaves them. Each of them is apparently no more than a memorial to the refusal of my discourse by the audience it included: an audience restricted to psychoanalysts.
> (Lemaire, vii)

Lacan, is of course, bemoaning here his misprision by the psychoanalytic establishment — or is he? As he continues, his commentary stages the kind of value-reversal that is so characteristic of his writing and which makes reading it one of the most rigorous exercises a critic can undertake. For although the implication of his failure to be recognised by mainstream psychoanalysis is certainly there, it is also the case that a second implication begins to take over: the question of the value of Lacan's psychoanalytic authority.

Lacan points out that his discourse 'included' his audience without 'retaining' it, like some sort of sieve, allowing (or forcing) his listeners to pass through it, rather than remain locked within it. In 'refusing' Lacan's discourse, his authority as the form of the social tie professor–student, Lacan's students (and here he also means the best of them) refused what he calls 'knowledge'. For Lacan this is not an error, but a move towards truth, since, in his vision, it is *knowledge* which has always been 'put in the place of the truth' (vii). In fact, speaking the truth is an impossibility since 'there is no knowledge without discourse', that is, outside of a 'form of a social tie', or what is currently labelled an 'institution'. A few paragraphs later he is discussing 'the segregation of psychiatry in the Faculty of Medicine' (viii), and psychiatry's double complicity with such segregation on the part of the university by its supplying a 'spare room' which he terms a 'ghetto' and which, he notes, was formerly an 'asylum'. And even though, he writes, 'a liberal *diktät* may arise there' it is the fact of boundary-creation and isolation that 'performs the office of social segregation' (viii). But even here the expected denunciation of all limits, of all boundaries, does not take place, for the refusal of segregation, he writes in a note, is 'basic to the concentration camp': the denial of limits is merely a *Verneinung* which does not undertake the critique from the standpoint of the *real*, of those 'discourses in which truth limps'.

It is Lacan's greatest genius to have given us a glimmering of what discourse, language, human life could be like without the mythification of limits, the mythification of metaphor, without, that is, the myths that always either overvalue those limits produced by metaphor, or dream of the ultimate apocalyptic overthrow of its power. He attempts to produce a discourse in which one can fall through its holes, transpire, in a sense, through its walls, without either negating or affirming them. (In another parlance Derrida will speak of hymens and thresholds, the tympanum, to image forth this transpiration.)

Even in these few lines, then, we have a great deal of Lacan: discursive practices, 'forms of the social tie', solidified as institutions, are the stuff of human knowledge, human culture, human life. Nothing 'human' exists outside their walls. Yet it is the walls themselves that must be questioned. 'Knowledge' is based on the ability to separate and make distinctions. But it is, Lacan finds, antithetical to the truth. And it is the 'truth' — the 'impossible' which Lacan calls the 'basis of the real' (viii) — that Lacan passionately pleads for. The trouble with institutions, discourses, is that they always imply limits, insides, outsides, they are based on negations ('determinations', as Spinoza named them), boundaries. Lacan calls this 'the inanity of the discourse of knowledge, which, asserting itself with its closure makes the others lie' (viii).

In all social forms based on language (especially in the form of a discourse of knowledge), truth, Lacan writes, 'limps', it is necessarily mutilated. As Lemaire puts it, for Lacan, 'Truth shies away from language' (40). Yet it is the truth Lacan is after. He calls for an impossible kind of half-speech in which the truth, while it still 'limps' as it does in all discourses, at least 'limps openly' (viii). What he is asking for is a kind of half-language which would be a 'real from within which the consistency of the discourses in which truth limps can be judged' (viii).

For Lacan, discourse is open to truth, which it can never contain, partly because it is overdetermined: the discoveries of the *epistème* are finally always only conveyed by *doxa* (40) or opinion, the expression of social values which will always frame, shape and play with the truth claims of knowledge. Lacan's own perverse technique for allowing the limping truth to be seen has been, he writes, to have engaged in 'midspeak' (*midire*), 'a technique which realises that the truth can only be half-spoken' (vii): 'La vérité . . . ne peut que se mi-dire' (*Scilicet* 6/7, 1976, 35). For Lacan, the psychoanalyst is never to show himself except in an 'asymptomatic discourse' (Lemaire, vii).

What does he mean by 'asymptomatic discourse'? What is 'midspeak'? How, specifically, does midspeak work? Lacan apparently feels that there is something in his teaching that escapes the awesome limits on truth imposed by the 'discourse of knowledge'. He claims that any analytical intervention should be ambiguous, equivocal, not theoretical, suggestive or imperative (*Scilicet* 6/7, 35). We know that his famous style, strangely ambiguous, even paranoid, has been dismissed by Derrida as so much froth covering over what he sees as Lacan's version of the 'truth' — the truth of castration and the missing member covered by the presence and unity of the phallus. And yet Lacan also sought to show why we invest so much in draping the genital act with the phallic veil. It is not so much because, as with the female body, the valued genital member *is* literally missing (thereby confirming the law of castration. Why, therefore hide it?), but because we do not wish to see it in anything but a symbolic, metaphorically arranged context. We never, writes Lacan, see the body as anything but a form, or figure. The 'truth' cannot be seen from within the context of the silent metaphor. On the other hand, the metaphor that makes itself seen, that draws attention to itself, *the symptom* (Lacan constantly makes the observation that a symptom is a metaphor in 'Du sujet enfin en question' — see Lemaire, 188; and EE, 175[5]), is a 'return of truth' even though it is within the 'order of the signifier' that it operates. 'Midspeak' names metaphor for what it is, rather than simply allowing its power to be exerted offstage. Midspeak promotes the 'truth', allows it to enter speech and the discursive form that had founded itself by excluding it. It enters in the places where we slip, fall through the cracks in 'discourse'.

Like one of Freud's nodal points, these few remarks introducing the text of another can be undone to reveal the manner in which the themes are knotted: authority, fiction and authorship, knowledge, institutions, boundaries, separation, choices, negation — and metaphor. And their absolute difference from the truth. For Lacan writes, in a line which is one of those strange keys he left lying around for a box with nothing inside it, that a symptom is a metaphor. And if the aim of analytic discourse is to be 'asymptomatic' we have found, perhaps, the thread of Ariadne by which we might begin to untie the knot.

Is, after all, the Lacanian effort to devalue 'knowledge' and the 'subject who is supposed to know' just some late-blooming romanticising of the simple? It is important to review a certain tradition — the one in which Lacan consciously inserts himself in order to deconstruct it — concerning the creation of discourse, the techniques of the exclusion of truth by means of knowledge. In this tradition, which includes not only Hegel, but Rousseau, Stendhal and Pascal, as well as Joyce, Lacan appears perhaps a different figure from what we have assumed. In order to read out his system I admit I have had to frame him with readings of others, of Freud, but also of Rousseau, especially the Rousseau of *The Second Discourse*. But I believe that I have sufficiently permitted Lacan to penetrate that frame.

I wrote this book because I was convinced, after reading through Lacan that he had a 'system'. I found that, as I read him, I began to be able to predict how he would handle certain themes, certain topics. But I was not at all convinced that his critics and analysts had adequately described that system. I am equally convinced that that system constituted an important new departure for examining, and perhaps beginning to cure, certain of the (unconscious) ills of cultural life.

I wanted to be able to demonstrate his system by my reading, but not the partial systems he had read, stolen from, borrowed — the systems of Saussure, Freud, Hegel, Benveniste, Lévi-Strauss, nor the 'systems' (actually legislated by the signifier) that he described as operating to shape culture: the SIR system (Symbolic Imaginary Real), Oedipus, grammar, economics. None of these systems, which he laid bare, *is* Lacan's system.

Like the international traveller who does not wish to be a 'mere' tourist, whoever crosses disciplinary borderlines, getting off the superhighways, the *grand'routes*, had better know different languages. They also have to have a method if their path is not already unfolded before them (method, Gr.: *meta* + *hodos*: above the path). In writing this book I have tried not so much to follow Lacan's path as to come before and after him. I look back to the literary and philosophical figures he so often cites and forward to those who have responded to him. My method has been to illustrate my points with literary, linguistic and social examples, and I feel that this is correct from a Lacanian viewpoint, which is a decentred, interdisciplinary one.

Notes

1. Stendhal, *Love*, tr. Gilbert and Suzanne Sale, Harmondsworth, Middlesex, Penguin, 1957.
2. Hereinafter all citations to the *Séminaires* will be in the text and will simply use the roman numerals *I, II, III, XI, XX*, followed by small numerals to indicate the seminar number (the only volumes that had appeared at the time of this writing). References to those seminars published as *The Four Fundamental Concepts of Psychoanalysis*, tr. Alan Sheridan, N.Y., W. W. Norton, 1978 (originally *Séminaire XI*, Paris, Seuil, 1973), will be cited as *4FC*.
3. Juliet Mitchell and Jacqueline Rose (eds.), *Feminine Sexuality: Jacques Lacan and the ecole freudienne*, New York and London: W. W. Norton, 1982, 1–57. Hereinafter 'Mitchell' in text citations.
4. Anika Rifflet Lemaire, *Jacques Lacan*, tr. David Macey, London, Boston and Henley, Routledge & Kegan Paul, 1977 (1st edn 1970).
5. References to the French edition of the *Ecrits*, Paris, Seuil, 1966,

will be cited in the text as FE: reference to the English translation, *Ecrits: A Selection*, tr. Alan Sheridan, New York and London, 1977, will be cited as EE. Other translations are mine.

Introduction:
Lacan's Literary Importance:
Reading *through* Lacan

In analytical discourse what it is always a question of is this — to that which pronounces itself by signifying you give a reading other than what it signifies.

(Lacan, 'La fonction de l'écrit', *II*, iii, 37)

The aim of this book is to assess critically the reasons for the growth of a Lacanian criticism, to track its diverse directions in the hands of his followers, and to try to give some sense of the contemporary historical reasons for Lacan's importance as a literary figure.

There is a well-known anecdote that Freud remarked to Jung, as they voyaged to America to lecture on psychoanalysis, that they were bringing 'the plague'. Lacan gives a new ending to this story. He writes that what Freud did not know when he pronounced those words was that, although the pair indeed did bring *la peste* to North America from Europe, America sent it right back, in the form of a distorted emphasis on the ego and its adaptation to the conditions of civilisation, especially the business-like civilisation of rational bureaucracy. Lacan never missed an opportunity to criticise the direction that the establishment of psychoanalysis in North America took — founded by immigrants who, of course, overemphasised adjustment and adaptation to their environment. In the country of self-reliance, how could one sustain a really serious critique of ego and identity? What is lost in the American translation is the heart and soul of psychoanalysis, the critique of the conditions and forms of limitation set by any civilisation, but the modern, economic[1] one in particular: 'she will think only of the income of her future husband'.

A certain passion for Lacan has now taken over literary studies in a way that calls for some assessment. It is interesting that, in distinction to the adventures of Freud on both sides of

1

the Atlantic and in relationship to Anglo-American culture, Lacan has managed, with relatively little delay, to have an impact simultaneously on French and Anglo-American culture, especially in its literary critical department. Use of his key concepts — the phallicised signifier in both semiotic and feminist criticism (Kristeva, Culler, Gallop, Mitchell), the gaze and suture in film studies (Mulvey, Berger), the figure and the body in deconstructive criticism (Derrida, de Man, Hartman, Spivak), transference in formalist criticism (Felman) — has touched nearly all the leading areas of literary criticism. Literature has responded to Lacan in a much more comprehensive manner than it did to the early uses of Freud for literature. For one thing, Lacan reverses the priorities, not reading literature in the light of Freud, but Freud as literature. While Lacan's influence has been greatest perhaps on those kinds of literary criticism already open to going beyond the narrow confines of literary purity, it is also the case that relatively formalist critics like Shoshana Felman, who was among the first to study and use Lacan (although her methods are closer to Freud), have found in Lacan a rich set of terms for formulating and formalising textual analyses. At the other extreme, studies oriented toward the 'social' rather than the 'literary' or 'psychological', even among Marxists like Jameson, find Lacanian terminology increasingly adaptable to and heuristic for their analyses, particularly in the study of ideology: the Other and the symbolic order appear with more and more frequency and now, almost, as a matter of course in such work. Even when critical distancing is expressed in his regard, nothing like either the wholesale adoption or rejection of Freud for criticism appears in the fate of Lacan and literature. Much more effective as a plague than Freud ever was, Lacan is everywhere and nowhere, like a contagion.

Now common to the vocabulary of nearly every important stream of literary critical activity, Lacan's words, his terminology, have found a ready response in the literary criticism of our time, as though filling a need it did not know it had until the means for satisfying it appeared. What is that need, and in what way does Lacan 'fill' it? Such questions are always best answered by looking first to areas of resistance, to those who deny the importance or decry the manner of his work.

Resistance to Lacan in literary criticism has not been nearly so emphatic as that to, say, Derrida or de Man. It appears chiefly among feminist critics who, sometimes killing the messenger who brings the bad news, protest against Lacan.[2] The protest is misdirected, of course, since they are more clearly protesting against the system Lacan exposed. But since any resistance at all always seems a good place for critical understanding to start, the feminist reaction is perhaps instructive.

It most certainly can be argued that the feminist reaction against Lacan is not just a special instance of simple obedience to the imperative that women, exhorted for centuries not to expose themselves, reflexively cover over the lack Lacan shows, weaving a phallus to hide the deficient pubis. (Such may be the case, say, of feminist reaction to something like the exposure pornography implies.) The feminist reaction to Lacan has been highly productive. In a mode quite different from the Oedipal rivalry generally assumed to be crucial to cultural creation, Lacan's reading by feminism has unleashed not a series of works designed to dethrone, decentre or deny Lacan but works dedicated to reformulating the imagery, the vocabulary and the network of associations attached to the figure of the woman. The great Soviet critic, Mikhail Bakhtin, pointed out that the best means of restructuring prevailing values is to make them the topic of discourse.[3] If so, then Lacan's presence as an impetus to Hélène Cixous's explicit formulation of the feminine as the dark continent, her rewriting of Oedipus from Jocasta's point of view, to Luce Irigaray's quest for a non-unified, non-phallic, but nevertheless specifically feminine figure — this sex which is not one, the divided locus of female sexuality — to Marguérite Duras's lucid reformulation of the masculine ideology as it destroys relationships in a work like *Maladie de la mort*, has been a factor in such a restructuring.

The criticism of those like Irigaray and Derrida (in many ways the feminist resistance, philosophical resistance, comes together in the work of Jacques Derrida and his circle, Philippe Lacoue-Labarthe, Jean-Luc Nancy and Sarah Kofman) depends heavily for its overall comprehension on the lack of fit between woman and the symbolic order that Lacan conveyed in his teaching. But even those critics who accuse Lacan of himself being a victim and apologist of phallogocentrism (in particular Derrida and his brand of feminism, but I must also count myself here)[4] find themselves nevertheless immersed in his terms, his words, writing about the same *topoi* he did.

For it is the commonplaces, the *koinoi topoi*, that Lacan challenges us to read. The commonplaces

— of everyday life (one seminar he gives is devoted to an analysis of a phrase in a letter of recommendation that someone is 'trustworthy');[5]
— of sacred texts (another essay is devoted to the Jehovan phrase: 'I am what I am', and its impact on the deletion of the position of the other, the 'you');[6]
— of philosophy (the effect of Aristotle's equation of the highest good with 'unmoved Being' on the love relation);[7]
— of science (was the Copernican Revolution really a revolution if it did not do away with the notion of the centre, but merely shifted its location from man to the sun?);[8]
— of social institutions like marriage (think of how terrifying the thought of 'two becoming one' really is, Lacan prompts us), or fatherhood (again showing how it is the thought of two becoming one that can terrorise with the tyrannical power metaphor has);[9]
— of the styles and forms of courtly love which have shaped the arrangement between the sexes (he calls courtly love simply the most elegant way we have found, by pretending the existence of obstacles, for covering up the impossibility of heterosexuality);[10]
— and finally, of the way in which commonplaces can be reevaluated, restructured, rewritten if not spoken. The classic locus for such revaluing is, of course, literature.

It is as though his richly allusive midspeak, his suggestions — and they are always posed as that, as suggestions, never as imperatives or directives — about which aspects of human being need to be reread (the sun, the centre, metaphor, the skin, the gaze, the highway) have captivated us all. Even in the act of resisting and criticising there is a major seductive power in Lacan's vocabulary, his style, his technique. It needs itself to be analysed, of course, but it also impels us towards seeing what else in the unconscious discourse, which is 'that which determines the form of a social tie', must urgently be analysed as well (*XX*, ii, 27).

Lacan's Literary Importance

To write or speak about someone generally requires taking a position or a point of view that transcends theirs, that allows one to frame them or place them somehow in a system. Lacan speaks about everything under the sun and calls it psychoanalysis. How can we frame him? Especially since he (along with Derrida's 'hymen' and 'parergon') fundamentally challenges the notion of the frame: in his Seminar of 11 May 1976 he tells the story of James Joyce, who one day is asked a question about an image which reproduces an aspect of the city of Cork. Joyce replies that it is Cork. The fellow says, I recognise it, but what is framing it? To which Joyce, who was waiting for this turn, replies: 'Cork' [*liège*] (*Ornicar?* 11, 1977, 5).

— Philosophically? By speaking about his speaking about the speaking being (*le parlêtre*), opening being to more and less than it *was*? Unlikely, since Lacan had much to say on the subject — the philosophical subject who is 'supposed to know' — and on the psychic twists that the fiction of a knowing subject entails. Psychoanalysis for Lacan transcends philosophy, though not in the expected direction (up).

— Scientifically? Science is supposed to be knowledge of the real, of that which, strictly speaking, exists outside (perhaps, science muses, only for the sake of) the mind and is devoid of significance. Yet Lacan finds that science is the 'science of little letters' ($e = mc^2$). Little letters, despite Descartes's dream of their neutrality, their absolute detachment, their pure availability for any symbolic ordering, a/b/c — have still become signifiers: of 'the scientific'. Even the numerical fails to resist significance: the cardinal system always, for the human being, takes on the values of the ordinal system (*4FC*, 226).

— Anthropologically, then? Yes, perhaps. After all, the mechanisms to which he has recourse (selection, combination, hierarchy, myth, mana, phallos) derive from anthropological conception and research. At times this discourse seems to be the key to Lacan, and early interpreters of his work certainly relied heavily upon his use of Lévi-Strauss.[11] For Lacan, discourse fundamentally determines the anthropological relation, the 'form of a social tie'. I can hardly stress enough how important the notion of the *social tie* is for Lacan. The fact that we generally are prepared to read psychoanalytic discussions as centred on an individual ego, from whose viewpoint all social and symbolic relationships are to be constructed and reconstructed must be rethought in the case of Lacan. Lacan supplemented the 'psychoanalytic ego' with the anthropological one, adopting the terminology of kinship and role that anthropology and linguistics utilised in order to demystify the ego. Lévi-Strauss, Benveniste, Jakobson all made the ego a shifter, a signifier (EE, 316) a place where intersections and crossroads of relationships meet.[12] Lacan questions more deeply, however:

> But where does this being [I/subject], who appears in some way defective in the sea of proper nouns, originate? We cannot ask this question of the subject as 'I'. He lacks everything needed to know the answer, since if this subject 'I' was dead, he would not, as I said earlier, know it.
>
> (EE, 317)

Lacan knew that Freud had discovered a fundamental disturbance in the interhuman circuit, the anthropological one. He could not leave unexamined the notion of even a merely 'virtual' centre such as the shifter implies: 'Topology indicates to us that, in a circle, there is a hole in the middle. One dreams over it, makes a centre of it, from whence all sorts of vocabulary effects' (*Ornicar?* 11, 1977, 4). He points out, in the 'Dialectic of Desire and Subversion of the Subject', how the Copernican Revolution failed fundamentally to dislocate the prestige of the centre: shifted from man and the earth to the sun, it is still the idea of the centre that controls discourse: 'heliocentrism is no less a lure than androcentrism' (FE, 797; EE, 165).

Lacan's critique of the individual ego was far further-reaching than this demystification. For Lacan criticised, before Derrida did, and in a very radical way that touched every aspect of human life, the notion of centring, of making the centre the point of view from which to assess and evaluate human being. Freud's discovery is that man is not completely in man. The fundamental human relation, Lacan tells us, cannot — as in the optimistic diagram of two persons that illustrates the human speech community which always accompanies Ferdinand de

Saussure's text — be reduced to two centres exchanging signals with each other (*III*, xxiii, 325: 'Grand'route/Être père'). Our relations, structured by the signifier, do not form an uninterrupted circle between me and you; instead they put us, Lacan writes, on a 'route', a path that goes towards the Other. Lacan offers an historical contrast between Hegel and Freud to illustrate why:

> Dans la perspective hégélienne, le discours achevé — sans doute, à partir du moment où le discours sera arrivé à son achévement, il n'y aura plus besoin de parler, c'est ce qu'on appelle les étapes post-révolutionnaires, laissons ça de côté — le discours achevé, incarnation du savoir absolu, est l'instrument de pouvoir, le sceptre et la propriété de ceux qui savent. (*II*, 89).
>
> [In the Hegelian perspective, completed discourse — doubtless, from the moment that discourse would have arrived at its end, there would no longer be any need to talk, it's what one calls the post-revolutionary stage — leave that aside — accomplished discourse, incarnation of absolute knowledge, is the instrument of power, the sceptre and the property of those who know.]

Hegel, Lacan claims, went beyond the religion of individualism grounded in a *tête à tête* with God, by showing that the reality of each human is in the being of the other. In his analysis of the social tie as the master–slave relation, Hegel reached the extreme edge of the anthropological circle. But 'Freud', Lacan writes, 'en a sorti' ('Freud got out of it').

Hegel, like Rousseau before him, had shown how, with the power arrangement of the master and slave and their co-dependence, interhuman relations move from the imaginary, the realm of prestige and the opinion of the other, into the symbolic; from the forms of 'love, contract, collaboration, passion and even the social contract including perversion' to the forms of 'struggle and work' (*I*, xviii, 249, 'L'Ordre symbolique'). All that social life had possessed of an imaginary dimension (what Lacan calls the 'love-link') is converted into the symbolic by a law, a law imposed on the slave. The imaginary, in which opinion and values are the key components, ceases to function properly in

7

the structure of mastery: the master enters into the relationship purely for prestige and at the risk of his life. And yet the recognition ('prestige') given the master by the slave is worthless — he is, after all, a mere slave. Therefore a new mode of organisation appears, a new form of social tie. A relationship between enjoyment and work appears. In relation to the master, it is no longer a question of the slave's being the conquered who lives by asking grace of the conqueror, but rather a question of his going to work, doing a job. And when one goes to work, it's a question of rules, hours — the symbolic domain. The slave, now a worker, submits not to the passion for prestige of the master, but to the law, the law that he is to satisfy the *desire and enjoyment* of the other.

These two modes — the imaginary and the symbolic — of social, interhuman life are not, Lacan insists, successive stages in humanity, but are intertwined. Although the symbolic disrupts the dual (actually binary) structure of the imaginary it also depends on it. The imaginary, close to the body and based upon its concrete topography, is the realm of passion, which Lacan defines closely as Spinoza did, as that in which man is open to division within himself. The domain of the 'béance' of human desire, in all its nuances, from 'shame to prestige, from buffoonery to heroism, by means of which human desire is entirely exposed to the desire of the other' (*I*, xviii, 246), the passions of the imaginary are, like these nuances, so many *cul de sacs* (247). And the *sac*, in Lacan's terminology is an image of the coming of the Symbolic.

Passions, for Lacan, are the passions of the ego; they are superseded only by the advent of the Symbolic. The Symbolic replaces the indexical topography of the body with the iconic imagery of geometry, the graph, the number, etc. Images displace, replace, the body, but their provenance is from the body: we take a feature, a trait, the surface of the skin. From there we move to the idea of the skin as a covering, and from there to that of a sack. From sack, we move to sphere, 'A sphere, this envelope in which we breathe supposes a cord which knots it' and all centring presupposes the 'logic of the sack and the cord' (*Ornicar?* 11, 1977, 5; see also *Scilicet* 6/7, 1976, 44; and *Ornicar?* 1–5, 1975, 90 on the 'géométrie du sac.'). In turn, however, the symbolic sphere does not remain untouched by the flatness and two-dimensionality of the imaginary, for we move from the sphere to *the circle*. And describing a circle is what makes a hole — a gap, *la béance* — in the centre.

Freud's discovery, Lacan tells us, 'that man is not completely in man', means that the fundamental human relation, structured by the signifier, the sexual relation, is skewed toward the Other. It is structured by the signifier which does not form an uninterrupted tie bonding us together, but only draws a circle around us. It draws a line *between* us and everything that *fails to signify*:

> My definition of a signifier (there is no other) is as follows: a signifier is that which represents the subject for another signifier. This signifier will therefore be the signifier for which all the other signifiers represent the subject; that is to say, in the absence of this signifier, all the other signifiers represent nothing, since nothing is represented only *for* something else.
>
> And since the battery of signifiers, as such, is by that very fact complete, this signifier can only be a line [*trait*] that is drawn from its circle without being able to be counted part of it. It can be symbolised by the inference of a (— I) in the whole set of signifiers.
>
> (EE, 316)

The signifier thus separates us from each other, disrupts any 'communication' we might have with each other. It also, he writes, puts us on a 'route', a path, that goes towards the Other. A third party lies outside this human world, this little economy (that which is in the circle has a certain non-value compared with the ultimate worth of what is beyond) which it has created, beyond any circular relationship between 'I' and 'you'. The signifier, drawing a circle around us, a boundary between us as 'speaking human beings' and 'all the rest', makes everything within the circle significant as well. But at a price, the price that this significance be removed from the circle, be relegated to an area beyond the circle. Thus it is itself absent or deleted from the circle itself.

E.g., *Bovary*

To give an idea, literarily, of how this notion of the signifier as a *'grand'route'* or superhighway works, and to give the idea, also, of how heuristic Lacan is for reading literature and its civilisation, let me turn for a moment to Flaubert's *Madame Bovary*. Emma Bovary is peculiarly bound by the circle of kinship (including its edges or margins) and the notion of a beyond that it offers. On the one side, her husband Charles, whose mother's highest aspiration for him is that he become a member of the Highway Department. On the other, Emma, drawn in her religious and other studies to the marginalia, the borders of the prayer books, the flowers that frame the religious ritual. Charles, content with the notion of the imaginary circle of his bourgeois life; Emma, feeling trapped in the circle, desiring to go beyond: how often the circular flounces of her dress spread around her on the floor make of her the bull's eye in a target.[13]

Each is equally caught in a circle not of their own making, and yet nevertheless not natural, a circle that presents itself not as a bounded limit, but as a highway, a progress. They differ only in their attitude towards it. It makes Charles feel safe, at home, 'leaning his elbows contentedly on the [round?] table of life'. Emma desires passionately to go beyond. No one has ever wanted so much for the signifier to have a signified than she: she will plunge her hand into and *eat* the arsenic in a move that can only be seen as the culmination of her quest. At last the mere signifier, the label 'dangerous' on Homais's arsenic, has come to have a real meaning. She will follow the highway, the phallic signifier writ at its largest (before the advent of the guided missile, perhaps), becoming a victim of the *drive* created purely by the signifier, which always promises meaning, satisfaction, but whose law is that it must not provide it. What Emma never realises is that it is the highway itself that has drawn the circle around her. So she takes Leon as a lover in a carriage that must 'Drive on!', but never get anywhere: the driver wonders, 'What mania for locomotion possessed these individuals that they should want to drive on for ever . . .' (251).

Listen to the speech of the Councillor at the Agricultural Fair at Yonville:

Let me be permitted, I say, to pay a fitting tribute to the Authorities, to the Government, and, gentlemen, to our beloved Monarch and Sovereign Lord the King, to whom no branch of public or private prosperity is indifferent, and who steers the chariot of state with a hand at once so firm and so wise, amid the ceaseless perils of a stormy sea — who knows, moreover, how to gain respect for peace no less than for war — for Trade and for Industry, for Agriculture and for the Arts . . .

I turn my gaze now to the present state of our fair land: what do I see? Everywhere trade and the arts flourish. Everywhere are new paths of communication, new arteries within the body politic, opening up new contacts. Our great manufacturing centres thrive once more [referring to things 'since the Revolution']. Religion finds new strength and smiles in every heart. Our ports are full. Confidence returns. At last France breathes again!

(155)

Determined by the particular discourse of bourgeois society that wishes to include everything *within* its borders, it is imperative that the routes, the highways remain open and flowing, so that (provided that one remains within it) this world can purport to satisfy any desire, even, perhaps, pre-empt desire.

Charles, for example, has an almost total lack of desire — if anything can characterise Charles it is his bovine inattention to desire. When, for example, he finds himself pleased at the thought of returning to old Rouault's farm, he thinks of it as the pleasure he feels when the gate scrapes his shoulder, not when he accidentally brushes up against Emma's body while he searches for his whip. Opposed to Charles in almost every particular, Emma is nothing but desire to go beyond the circle. This desire, the *'grand'route'* to the Other, is entirely structured by the initial drawing of the boundary lines around her. Her desire is to get beyond the narrow circle of her existence, but she must proceed in this ironic effort according to the rules of the game. Unlike her greyhound who, as Tony Tanner puts it, simply wanders off and out of it,[14] Emma struggles with the circle on its own terms. Thinking to eschew the circle, she chooses the highway, but as in all stories of desire structured by the Other, the line is drawn

11

into a circle, and Emma remains trapped within it.

Lacan has described the dialectic of desire as a 'desire to return to the inanimate margin beyond life that language gives to the human being by virtue of the fact that he speaks'. Emma Bovary, with the gender carefully changed, fulfils this definition.

Lacan is always alert to the possibility of breaking a circle. But the circle he is anxious to disrupt is not only, as everyone emphasises, the specular mother−child relationship, but the circle drawn *around* humanity and *between it* and all the rest by signification, a signifying process that locates its origin or source beyond the circle rather than through discourse — the form of a social tie.

> What is suggested here [is] that it is structural of the subject, it constitutes in it essentially that margin that all thought has avoided, skipped over, circumvented, or blocked whenever it seems to succeed in being sustained by a circle, whether that circle be dialectical or mathematical.
>
> (EE, 318)

Anxious to show that the imaging of a circle depends on the line, the trait, the phallic signifier, Lacan enjoys disrupting the circle of the imaginary with the symbolic. But what does this mean? That he opts for a 'god', a prime signifier who lies 'beyond' the circle and is absent from it?[15] Hardly, since it is only the fact of the sacrifice of the relationship of self and other, the pleasure of this association that creates the fiction of a circle at all. Lacan writes that joy, the joy of union with the 'beyond' of the circle, is barred by pleasure:

> For it is pleasure that sets the limits on *jouissance*, pleasure as that which binds incoherent life together, until another, unchallengeable prohibition arises from the regulation that Freud discovered as the primary process and appropriate law of pleasure.
>
> (EE, 319)

The reader should note how Lacan reverses the value emphasis

12

so that when joy, with its purposely religious overtone, is unattainable it is the 'fault' of pleasure, whereas it is clearly that the law demands we sacrifice, give over as a 'gift' to human civilisation, Freud's *Kultur*. In short, even the pleasure of association is dominated by a cultural principle which demands its being driven toward cultural aims, or rather, toward *the* only real aim of civilisation — the drive to reproduce — itself. As a principle of its organisation, culture demands the sacrifice of pleasure for this 'higher' aim. The trouble is, Lacan finds, that the purely symbolic principle is never apprehended except through the imagination:

> We must distinguish . . . between the principle of sacrifice, which is symbolic, and the imaginary function that is devoted to that principle of sacrifice, but which, at the same time, masks the fact that it gives it its instrument.
>
> (EE, 319)

The 'symbolic' principle is as dependent on the image, the signifier, as the imagination is on the symbolic:

> [The castration complex] is the only indication of that *jouissance* of its infinitude that brings with it the mark of its prohibition, and, in order to constitute that mark, involves a sacrifice: that which is made in one and the same act with the choice of its symbol, the phallus. This choice is allowed because the phallus, that is, the image of the penis, is negativity in its place in the secular image. It is what predestines the phallus to embody *jouissance* in the dialectic of desire.
>
> (EE, 319)

Literature helps us to read Lacan as much as the reverse.

So if the scientific and the anthropological or human sciences and the philosophical definitions of human being are subjected by Lacan to a radical critique because of their anchoring in the discourse of the centre, then the only logical alternative mode for discourse about this discourse is literary or rhetorical. The argument may be made, for Lacan, that psychoanalysis and literature are two names for his fundamental critique of the egocentric, androcentric point of view. Implying, of course, that

13

the decentred point of view would have to conceive of the 'form of a social tie' — of discourse — very differently from the way in which that discourse has been conceived until now.

Tout le reste est littérature.

Lacan says, in fact, that everything is literature.

It is *literature* and not language or linguistics that is the proper model for figuring Lacan. Although it has been the usual practice to apply structuralist versions of language to Lacan and to reduce his method to the metaphor/metonymy opposition, it is not enough to do so without also paying strict attention to the form of the social ties these figures make. Moreover, the implications of metaphor for Lacan are so profound (we are in metaphor and unlikely to get out of it alive) that we can characterise human life as fundamentally not so much linguistic as literary. What understanding the role of the figure in Lacan amounts to is a reconception of the figure along non-Hegelian lines; specifically, along the lines that deconstruction, *à la* de Man and Derrida, has taught us. Such a reconception requires that we reformulate the figure beyond the limits imposed by a closed system[16] (*'le discours achevé'*), although even putting it in these terms is crudely incorrect, since in the figure as developed by Lacan, there is neither an inside nor an outside to language and in fact it is the idea of self-imposed limits that is perpetually at issue in his texts. In other words we do not, in Lacan, have a sense that we are trapped in the prison-house of language, whose opposite would be silence, animality, Kristevan *jouissance*:[17] In fact the contrary is the case, since it is precisely this fiction of an outside, an unmoved Being, that Lacan pinpoints as the source of our woes. Rather, in Lacan we have to come to terms with language on language's terms. And that entails erasing borderlines and interpenetrating 'categories' in such a way that they no longer produce absolute division and separation, the hierarchical end-products of metaphorical selection.

The following sections specify the functions of metaphor in Lacan and how it touches every aspect of human being. Here, I only wish to note that Lacan indeed commented often and directly upon Derrida, mentioning on several occasions that he had 'shown Derrida the way' (*Ornicar?* 11, 1977, 3). And if nothing else, he clearly showed the way to 'White Mythology' which we can now use as a guide for rereading Lacan. What is less well known, interestingly, is Lacan's comment that it was Paul de Man who had managed to 'frayer ma route aux Etats Unis', and felt that he and de Man were 'doing the same thing' (*Scilicet* 6/7, 1976, 48). Since Lacan's life-long struggle was, in many senses, a struggle with the ideologisation of psychoanalysis that had occurred under the sign of the dollar, such a *frayage*[18] must have appeared in his eyes as no small accomplishment. Thus my reading of Lacan is marked by the so-called poststructuralist perspective: it is as if, as Freud would have been able to predict, we could read Lacan only in the mode of *Nachträglichkeit*, that is by tracking his spoor through deconstruction — a term he himself concocted.[19]

Notes

1. 'Le capitalisme se marque par un certain nombre d'effets, qui sont des symptômes; c'est un symptôme dans la mesure où Marx impute à l'humanité d'avoir une norme, et il choisit la norme prolétaire (*Scilicet*, 24 Nov. 1976, 34). Lacan showed no overt political alignments in his writing, but it is certain that he looked toward major reformulations of social institutions.

2. For a detailed (if critical) report on the French feminist responses by Michèle Montrelay, *L'Ombre et le nom*, Luce Irigaray, *Speculum de l'autre femme*, and Eugénie Lemoine, *Partage des femmes*, see Marie Christine Hamon, *Ornicar?* 11, 1977, 37–47. She stresses the importance of their analyses, but believes they fail to understand the substance of the psychoanalytic approach as one that treats *form* and *value*. Women often make elisions in quotations from Lacan, or cite him in pieces that distort the overall reading he is giving of women (see Larysa Mykyta, 'Lacan, Literature and the Look', *Sub-stance*, xxii:2, 1983, 49–57). There is much confusion about Lacan's position toward women; clearly he radicalised our awareness of the relative value of women in our culture, showing its basically negative sign. But it seems to me his effort was toward reframing this value: so that everything he writes about women that may seem 'negative' becomes in his system, 'positive', a relative freedom from the impasses the phallic male is trapped in. Both Juliet Mitchell and Jacqueline Rose have reread Lacan in this latter way in their introductions to *Feminine Sexuality*.

3. I have analysed Bakhtin's work on value in 'The Temporality of Textuality: Bakhtin and Derrida', *Modern Language Notes*, Dec. 1985.

4. In a chapter ('Phallacious Theories of the Subject') of my earlier

book, *The Time of the Sign*, W. Dean MacCannell (Bloomington, Indiana, Indiana University Press, 1982), I had responded similarly to Lacan's insight about phallic hegemony in our culture.

5. *Les Seminaires de Jacques Lacan : I, Les Ecrits techniques de Freud*, Paris, Seuil, 1975, xviii, 254 ff.

6. Lacan distinguishes the Biblical God from that of Aristotle because Jehovah is definable only by means of enunciation (*'Je suis celui qui suis'*) rather than by spatial and geometric images (he sees the Greek god as defined as a non-verbal, fixed sphere). In *III (Les Psychoses)*, xxiii, pp. 323−4, Lacan shows how the Jehovan assertion radically undermines — because verbal — claims to absoluteness: if we listen to the voice, it says 'I am who I am', but it can also say 'I am he who follows' (*être* versus *suivre* as the verb of *suis/suit*). It is for this reason that Lacan calls him an 'atheist', hidden God, thrown into ambiguity by the fact of his speech.

7. *XX (Encore)*, vi, pp. 61−71, Paris, Seuil, 1975; this seminar is also translated in Mitchell, 137−48. Lacan works toward a redefinition of love as ruled neither by the forms of *agapé*, nor narcissism, nor *filia*.

8. He points out, in the 'Dialectic of Desire and Subversion of the Subject', how the Copernican Revolution failed to dislodge the prestige of the centre: it shifted from man and the earth to the sun, but it is still the idea of the centre that controls discourse (EE, 295; FE, 797; also EE, 165, and *XX*, iv, 42: 'Far from being shaken by this discovery that the earth was not the centre, he substituted the sun for it'). For Lacan, Kepler was more radical than Copernicus in his thinking of the ellipsis, which has no centre, rather than the circle (*XX*, 43); with Copernicus, the conception of the world remains spherical, and therefore only a deduction of the ego-sphere.

9. 'The Signification of the Phallus', EE, 281−91; FE, 685−96; also *III*, xxiii, 329−31.

10. Mitchell, 141 and *XX*, vi, 65. Lacan writes that we need to re-evaluate courtly love since it was 'the only way of coming off elegantly from the absence of sexual relation'.

11. Anthony Wilden's *System and Structure: Essays in Communication and Exchange*, London, Tavistock, 1972 is still the most complete explication of Lacan in English; esp. chs. I, II and IV. When he moves into the study of general culture, he tends to leave Lacan behind, using Lévi-Strauss extensively in ch. IX and on phallus in exchange (268).

12. See Lévi-Strauss's *Myth and Meaning*, N.Y., Schocken Books, 1978: 'I never had, and still do not have, the perception of feeling my personal identity. I appear to myself as the place where something is going on, but there is no "I", no "me". Each of us is a kind of cross-roads where things happen' (4−5).

13. Gustave Flaubert, *Madame Bovary*, tr. Alan Russell, Harmonds-worth, Middlesex, Penguin, 1951, 141.

14. Tony Tanner, *Adultery in the Novel*, Baltimore and London, Johns Hopkins University, 1979, 299, details the circles in the Flaubert

novel. My references are to the English of the Penguin paperback edition.

15. See note 6 above. Dialoguing with those (Philippe Lacoue-Labarthe and Jean Luc Nancy) who had accused his 'Other' of being the 'good old God of Aristotle' in 'Dieu et la jouissance de femme', Lacan writes that it was that good old god he was trying to exorcise (Mitchell, 152–5), that is, the idea of Being as a fixed, unmoved sphere, toward which the soul, which had fallen away from that sphere, moves impelled by a desire that is 'a will to joy' (FE, 773). For Lacan, the 'unmoved' god is the 'manifestly mythical' origin of the soul (âme). This soul comes into being by differentiating 'woman' from it; it is by means of the soul that love for being (which is only self-love magnified) limits love to 'souling' — âmour.

16. I have written on the problem of the figure in terms of the difference between a closed and open system in 'Kristeva's Horror', Semiotica (forthcoming).

17. For Lacan, 'joy' is what we give to the Other, it is surplus value. He also claims that it is always in the shape of phallic jouissance. What Lacan means by this is that joy — enjoyment — exists only within certain limits (the space of joy is 'bounded', XX, i, 13), it figures a certain geometry which regulates joy (XX, i, 14). Given over to the Other, enjoyment is deferred absolutely for ourselves. Women, for Lacan, are not caught up in this delivering of joy to Being for many reasons, one of which is that women's bodies are the site of a disconnection between sexual pleasure and reproduction. Lacan puns on the French term 'enjoy' as an imperative ('jouis!') because it is the way in which the subject 'hears' (j'ouis) its castration by the sur-moi (XX, 13). Also in the seminar on Jakobson (XX, ii, 27): 'What is not a sign of love is the joy of the Other.' In the following chapters I discuss the difference between the sign and the signifier.

18. 'Facilitated my access'. Frayage is the usual translation of Freud's Bahnung, and it is used in relation to the mark made by an impulse on the nerve.

19. Lacan gave his seminar on 'The Deconstruction of the Drive' 6 May 1964 (4FC, 161–73).

1

The Critical Response: Readings
of Lacan

In setting out to write this book I was first guided by the critical response to Lacan, and thus to the way in which Lacan's discourse has been 'returned' to him (if it has been) by its 'addressees'. For while he overtly spoke to analysts and would-be analysts, the critical response, from literature and philosophy, indicates that it was not limited to this particular group. We must ask what, in his discourse, refused to restrict itself to being received only by those with special knowledge?

An overview of the responses to Lacan by his critics provides only a partial answer, but that answer is a beginning. In this section I set forth the major readings of Lacan in a way that demonstrates not only the depth and variety of those who listened to him but also an interesting pattern of reading — what Paul de Man would have picked out as an instructive blindness: this blindness that will help us in our effort to lay bare Lacan's 'system'.

My aim 'to lay bare Lacan's system' may seem odd in this era of anti-systems, and particularly given that the kind of 'system' Lacan works at, very much in the spirit of Freud, is a resistance to system.

In demonstrating such a resistance in Lacan my reading, of course, goes against the grain of the majority of those — enthusiasts and critics alike — who have responded to Lacan. The pattern of these responses has been to study his systems: the SIR system (Symbolic Imaginary Real); the L schema:

(S-----o
o' ----)

18

and the algorithms, patriarchal ideology, Saussurean semiology, Jakobsonian rhetorical analysis, Freud's Oedipal schema, Hegel's dialectic of desire and self-consciousness, Lévi-Straussian anthropology; Benveniste's linguistics, etc.: and to attribute them *to* Lacan, to assert that each one of the partial systems I mention here *is* Lacan's system.

The tendency, that is, of his readers has been to over-identify Lacan's analysis of the culture of the signifier with Lacan, with his own stance *on* that culture. The systems that are formed by the signifier, the field of the Other, the Symbolic Order, the gender economy, the circle, the heliocentric universe, etc. are entirely, thoroughly, tirelessly worked out by Lacan: no analyst was ever more complete in his examination of his patient, which is, in Lacan's case, culture itself. But just as the physician may be said to be apart from the disease s/he discovers, even if s/he has been constrained by it, Lacan's analysis of the systems formed by the signifier, metaphor, the phallus, stand apart from his own 'system'.

Not that uncovering his system is made easy in his work — he is trying to renew the way we think, act and live *form*; he wants to get out of the circle, the logic, that speech has given us over to. As such his own forms are unfamiliar to us. The forms we know, rooted in language, as Husserl once said, as the first forming principle, were exactly what Lacan sought to re-form. If he wants to get away from the circle, what does he 'put in its place' — the ellipse? Yes, since, his writings could be formally characterised as elliptical not only in the rhetorical sense but in terms of their content: he is concerned with remains, with what is left out, or left over. He also characterises the ellipse as radically different from the circle because it has no centre (see Intro., note 8). But much more importantly, from the perspective I have taken in this book, none of the geometric forms he was so fond of illustrating his lectures with remain signifiers for him. If, for example, he schematises the family circle (at least in the cheerful version of Oedipus) as a quadrangle (Mother :: son as Father :: daughter), he shows how it becomes a triangle whose three angles are separated from each other, held apart and at a distance by the depression of the fourth point, the Mother. The Borromean knots were his attempt at a new geometry, un-separating the three angles of the Oedipal triangle, but also as an opening to analysis, from the point of view of the widest possible cultural context, of the 'mental fabrications whose instrument is the mathematical symbol'.[1]

His 'forms', then, are not the ones we are accustomed to dealing with — any well-worn route is, after all, a track made by the signifier. It is the challenge of thinking new forms, of thinking them through with Lacan, thinking them apart from the Other, knowledge, metaphor, patriarchy, the drive etc., that makes reading Lacan an exciting and — to my mind — a crucial undertaking, crucial for the shape of modern culture.

The Readings of Lacan: The Philosophers

One might assume that the readers best able to systematise and synthesise Lacan's thought would be philosophers, especially philosophers of the sort his writing calls for: those who mix genres, 'literary' and 'conceptual' language, the deconstructionists.

A case could certainly be made for Lacan's claim that everything in Derrida is already in his work; Derrida, despite 'Le facteur de la vérité', has followed a career path that has taken him quite literally down Lacan's 'track': retreading Hegel and Kant in *Glas* in the light of Lacan's attempt to counter Oedipus with Antigone; emphasising metonymy in the work on Edmond Jabès; writing on the irreducibility of metaphor and the sun in 'La mythologie blanche'; and listening more closely to the ear of the Other.[2] The question is whether he has travelled this 'track' in an opposing direction.

I think not, at least if we attend to Derrida's effort to disrupt the very forms in which his discourse is given, which certainly follows Lacan's direction. Of course, there is confusion on this point as Derrida's relation to Lacan enters the critical scene by virtue of a sharp attack on Lacan for his purveying of truth.[3] Derrida rebels at Lacan's apparent assertion of the hegemony of, the truth of, the law of castration and of the unity of the phallus. His cogent critique is highly applicable to what Derrida calls the psychoanalytic 'edifice' built upon this unity. But his rebellion is mis-aimed in the case of Lacan, who, as I show, calls, if not for rebellion (for him futile) then at least for

20

resistance to this kind of 'truth', this kind of 'law'.

Lacan emphasised, to be sure, that we must recognise the awesome power — for him, the power of life and death — of the signifier, the phallus, to shape our existence. But this does not necessarily make him its partisan, although the fact that so brilliant and sophisticated a reader as Derrida at first responds to him in this way shows how effective Lacan's proof of this power is. In short, the critique does not, ultimately, apply to Lacan. Lacan calls for a 'limping truth' (discussed above and in FE 786). This 'limping truth' is not simply a reiteration of the 'truth' of the paternal metaphor, the 'truth' that only shows itself by hiding what is most essential. The phallic truth is precisely that against which Lacan re-writes every line — in its metaphoric hegemony, its fiction of unity, its creation of 'oneness'.

Derrida's work has amply demonstrated his opinion of Lacan's terms, and I shall return to this aspect of their interesting relationship in later chapters. But the pattern of reading holds true for two other highly sophisticated readers of Lacan, Philippe Lacoue-Labarthe and Jean-Luc Nancy, to whose book, *Le Titre de la lettre: lecture de Lacan* (1973), Lacan replied in his essay on the *jouissance* of women (*XX*, vi, 62 and *passim*). In a series of critical readings of Lacan's treatment of the letter, the literal letter, Lacoue-Labarthe and Nancy manage to repeat what Lacan said was most problematic about the rule of the signifier — although they deny that he saw any problems with it. For example, on pages 110–17 the two take the image of the circle in Lacan, analyse it, and then diagram the ' "Système" de *l'Instance de la lettre, ou: De revolutionibus orbium litteralium*' (this last phrase, a quote from Lacan's *Radiophonie*). Showing the circularity of the system in 'L'Instance', the two young philosophers also show circles within circles, and demonstrate how the 'irreducible duality' of the metaphor/metonymy opposition itself closes the circle (113).

Turning their graphic realisation of the circularity of Lacan's discourse into a genuine transcendence of it, the two 'discover' that the circle they describe *is* Lacan's system.

Lacan (his thought, his identity) is, they find, himself caught in the circle:

Mais la circulation d'une telle 'identité' exige, pour son cercle, un *centre*. C'est dans cette nécessité du centre que l'on peut voir la figure qu'est le schéma exercer la constrainte la plus décisive sur ce qu'elle figure. Dans la mesure, en effet, où un tel graphisme rend commodément mais correctement compte du discours de Lacan, ce discours s'avère du même coup comme *circulaire* c'est-à-dire comme systématique. Mais il s'avère donc aussi comme *centre*, alors même que le graphisme n'a pas pu (et pas dû) inscrire ce centre en effet. (114–15)
[But the circulation of such an 'identity' requires, for its circle, a *centre*. It is in this requirement for a centre that one can see a figure like this schema exercise the most decisive constraint over what it figures. In so far, in fact, as such a graph takes into account easily but correctly Lacan's discourse, this discourse avows itself, by the same token as *circular* — that is, as systematic. But it avows itself also as *centred*, even though the graph has not (and should not have) inscribed this centre in fact.]

How ironic their triumph. No figure in literary history — except, perhaps for Rousseau (and, in modern criticism, Paul de Man) — has ever had to bear being so mistaken for the pathologies they depict. *The* critical issue in Lacan is exactly whether his demonstration of the power of the signifier to create signification, to centre, to draw circles ever more tightly around human beings and between them and all the rest, between the one and the All, is the same thing as his own meaning. To have uncovered a structure does not, as I shall show, make him a partisan of the process of signification, any more than the lab report that describes the presence of a lethal organism is on the 'side' of the malignant element: Lacan, let us not forget, is a doctor.

The particular charm of Lacan's way of responding to the other, his seductive manner, is illustrated by the way he chose to frame his response to Lacoue-Labarthe and Nancy. He follows the seminar, which develops the themes of his answer (*XX*, vi), with another (vii) whose title must be read as responding to the title of 'the title of the letter': 'Une lettre d'amour' (*I*, vii, 73–82; Mitchell, 160, deletes this dialogue).

To be fair to philosophy: one of the other 'philosophers' who has read Lacan closely and written about him is a woman, and her reception of Lacan differs from that of the fellows I have just cited; it is sympathetic. Catharine Clément's book *The Lives and Legends of Jacques Lacan*[4] ought to be read by those who want a more social sense of Lacan, of the Paris scene, by those who wonder why, for example, his seminars are reported to have drawn the most beautiful and intelligent women in Paris as students. A feminist, a socialist and a Jew, Clément writes about Lacan in a way that should be revealing to people from each of those 'persuasions' who have questioned him fundamentally from within their different camps.[5] She works to give a sense of Lacan's importance to women, of his opening those questions about our assumptions of woman's place, woman's desire that even some of his other students (both male and female, e.g. Schneiderman and Kristeva) have not necessarily seen: she stresses how Lacan comes to analysis because of his interest in 'The Ladies' Way'.

Where Clément's reading falls short, it seems to me, is not in her over- or undersystematising Lacan, but in her resistance to thinking through what is a radical departure, the rearrangement of things Lacan's critique of the culture of the signifier calls forth. She tells us that she dropped out of the seminars after a while, going back briefly during the stresses of Lacan's last dissolution of his 'school'. For her, he is or was 'past', a neo-Kantian thinker who reasoned in the midst of his passion: her term for his work is 'aesthetic distance'. But distance from what? My sense is that the distance he called for is a distance *on* the aesthetic, the way that we have ceded ourselves to the aesthetic. Not the *fact* that we have done so, but our manner: if whatever is unspeakable is replaced by an image at the same time it is rejected into the real (EE, 183), Lacan writes, 'the problem is not in the reality that is lost, but in what takes its place' (EE, 188–9). Clément's Lacan ends as an aporia; she characterises him as an androgynous shaman (Clément, 202). I am not convinced that Lacan would have 'placed' himself in the particular relationship of self to Other and to other that this ambiguous personage occupies.

The Practitioners of the Linguistic Arts

There have been some rather interesting career trajectories among Lacan's students — certainly, every major figure in French intellectual life of the last 30 years was touched by him in important ways: Barthes, Foucault, Kristeva, Sollers, Althusser, Mannoni, Ricoeur, Derrida *et al.* attended his seminars; his close friends included surrealist poets, movie stars (including his wife)[6] and the great Structuralists, Lévi-Strauss, Jakobson and Benveniste. I have become intrigued, however, by those students whose disciplinary 'base' (e.g. linguistics or history or anthropology) has been fundamentally revalued by Lacan, and who have chosen, therefore, to forsake their original field for the field of psychoanalysis. I think looking at them is important because they reflect a growing trend in the humanities toward psychoanalysis, particularly in those fields devoted to the language arts: linguistics and literary criticism. The frequently-offered rationale for leaving them and going into psychoanalysis is the idea of *practice*, of getting out of the prison-house of language by getting in touch with patients, with those who suffer.

Among those who made the move are those who became Lacanian analysts, having submitted themselves to the peculiar anti-institutional regime that Lacan's *École* and sub-*écoles* demanded of the would-be practitioner. Stuart Schneiderman, a former Professor of Literature in the United States, is a prominent example. His book, *Jacques Lacan: Death of an Intellectual Hero*, gives the most detailed account, in English, of the method of training in the *École*, and of those forms peculiar to it: especially the Pass.[7] In the Pass, the analyst who wanted to be certified as an A.E. (*analyste de l'école*), in contrast to the A.M.E. (*analyste membre de l'école*; pp. 65–6), was required to determine when he or she thought the end of his or her own analysis had been reached. As Lacan described it, the *passe* begins when 'someone feels ready to take on patients, and tells a peer what gave him the nerve to think so' (*Scilicet* 6/7, 15). At that point, the candidate's analyst selected, for him or her, two or three other candidates for the same degree whom it was felt would qualify as stand-ins for the candidate. The candidate then was to discuss with those selected the reasons why he or she felt their analysis had correctly been terminated. After that, one of the substitutes (the candidate never knew which) was to stand for the candidate, to speak for him or her before a committee, which decided whether to pass or fail — 'The candidate himself never went before the committee' (Schneiderman, 68).

Schneiderman tells us that this particular institution was a failure, 'horrifying' to the factionalised students, who, in Schneiderman's account, assumed those who spoke on one's behalf were 'expected to be in the position of rivals' (69). His story of the *École* is done in highly individualistic and culture-bound terms: he concentrates on the rivalries, hostilities and minor politics of the conflicting faculties; he interprets the Lacanian hostility toward American psychoanalysis as having nothing to do with either theory or practice, but with a 'them' vs. 'us' problem, wherein all the paranoia is concentrated on the side of the French. Which is why he fails to understand the Pass in the context of Lacan. Schneiderman seems unable to pinpoint the rationale for the Pass.

Lacan, he writes, instituted the Pass in order to occupy the place of the Other (81), to be able to demand of the potential analyst who he was, what he was doing, how he got where he was (81). But when he attempts to tell us why Lacan thought of thinking up such a bizarre form, he gives us a set of overlapping and confusing reasons, each based on aspects of Lacan's reading of the *systems of the signifier*, not, my argument is, Lacan's 'system'. Schneiderman speculates that the peculiar ritual of the Pass stems from the would-be analyst's having had his destiny already estalished elsewhere than where he lives. Or from the fact that the analyst is supposed to be 'characterised by silence' and is thus taken by the patient 'as coming from the dead'. Or, he guesses again, the Pass will develop how 'the analyst speaks from the place attributed to him in the transference' (69–70). Maybe, Schneiderman wonders, there are two passers because 'signifiers always come in pairs'.

He concludes with an elaborate structure, linking the Pass to 'a psychoanalytic version of the last judgement' (69–70) a judgement that, if one passes, leads not to Heaven and eternal life, but to the particular, the peculiar 'joy' of being subjected to this judgement: sacrifice, responsibility, duty and death (70). Connecting the Pass to sex and to the supersession of sex by the death drive, the triumph of death — for him, the deferral of satisfaction, experienced as a 'joy'; for Schneiderman, 'the intense pleasure of orgasm' (74) — Schneiderman reaches the 'truth' — the Oedipal truth, the same one Freud taught.

Let us mark Schneiderman's equation of sex and death, sexual *jouissance* as pleasure that gives death. One should wonder why it is, for him, Oedipus legislates the Pass.[8] Is his ultimately the (American) bias towards adaptation? How disproportionate can the relation of theory and practice be? Why institute the Pass, when other social and cultural rituals always return to Oedipus? And why, if this is what is going on, does the Pass, at least in Schneiderman's account, fail?

For Schneiderman the Pass fails because a self-conscious subject (the candidate) is unwilling 'to be in a place that symbolises death' (72), 'through a renunciation of narcissism' (80). It is this renunciation that the analyst as *'le mort'* (the dummy in bridge) must make.[9] Schneiderman translates the renunciation of the ego as its absorption and identification with the Other: the analyst becomes, if not quite God, at least an oracle. He depicts Lacan as having made such a self-identification:

How did the Pass come to pass? Lacan must have asked himself the question: Why would anyone ever become a psychoanalyst? And when the question took this form, Lacan probably thought to himself that he did not have the answer. The question is a simple one, perhaps too simple [but evidently not simple enough for Schneiderman not to have overlooked Lacan's statement about the unhappiness of the arrangement between the sexes: JFM] for us to torture our minds over it, but the answer is far from self-evident. Perhaps Lacan one day, sitting in his analyst's chair, waiting for the next patient, found himself faced with the questions: What am I doing here, how did I get here, and why did I want to be here? Instituting a ritual was Lacan's way of posing this question for others, asking them to respond to it. Lacan never promoted himself as having all the answers. At best he was a questioner, at times acting like a Zen master, becoming himself a splendid enigma. Within the confines of his theory this place was that of the Other, the capital Other or the grand Other. Those he called his students felt themselves obliged to respond, to offer answers, most of which this Other found not entirely satisfying.

(82)

For Schneiderman, the only counter to the individual ego is the superego who judges, and judges negatively: the superego that Lacan is, in this description, mimicking. Thus Schneiderman's depiction of the Parisian scene of psychoanalysis as a conflict of narcissistic egos subsumed only by an 'above-it-all' Lacan flows logically from his perception, and may, for all I know, be an accurate reflection of his perception, but it reflects nothing of the theory that was supposed to shape this particular practice.

Lacan once said that the failure to sustain praxis ('a concerted human effort to treat the real by the symbolic' (*4FC*, 6)) results in the 'exercise of power' (EE, 226). If we put the emphasis on the term 'concerted', we might begin to think through 'the Pass' as a form of social tie.

There is a number of *Ornicar?* (12, 1977) in which Lacan speaks of the Pass (*sém.*, 3 November 1973, 117–23). Here he claims the Pass is motivated by an attempt to *revise the principles* by which any human group is situated in the real. He wanted to place, among those who studied in his institute, peoples 'whose presence alone among them totally changed the scope [*portée*, significance] of this title [A.E.]':

> C'est là ce qui se produit dans tout agrégat humain quand les êtres recrutés se situent dans ce réel au nom de principes tout différents de ceux qui ont permis auparavant de constituer une classe. Le fait que cette classe, gardant le même nom, est habitée par un tout autre type d'individus, est susceptible de changer tout à fait, non pas certaines structures fondamentales, mais la nature du discours. (117)

[That's what happens in any human group when beings recruited to it situate themselves in this reality in the name of principles entirely different from those which formerly permitted the constitution of a class. The fact that this class, retaining the same name, is inhabited by a completely other type of individual, is susceptible to changing altogether, not certain fundamental structures, but the nature of discourse.]

Which is to say, therefore, capable of changing the arrangements, if not the foundations, under which they speak with each other.

Lacan's effort was quite frankly to disrupt the prestige, the presence and the power of the Other taken as a form of ego, even a superego. If the analyst was to become a kind of substitute 'Other' it was only in the mode of an ironic subversion of the Other modelled as an ego. The 'two egos' model of the interhuman fails because there is, literally, no *other* involved in its imagined situation. Any desire for symmetricality and exchange is already an appeal to the Other to sanction and guarantee the equality invoked; it will always be only a misrepresentation of the real situation, which is one of mastery and subjection. In this context, we could read the Pass not as a 'last judgement' but as a refusal to render a 'last judgement' — at least not one that the would-be analyst ever 'hears'. 'The analyst must not hear voices,' Lacan writes, both playfully and seriously, and ambiguously (*4FC*, 258). The Pass is, perhaps, an effort to disrupt the fiction that analysis has to do with the *ego* of either the analysand or the analyst. As Lacan once wrote of de Sade, in comparing him with Kant, he is honest, because he overtly speaks desire through the voice of another, rather than pretending to do so through the 'I'. It is this kind of 'honesty' in the relationship to the Other that Lacan's *passe* seems to me to have been striving for.

It is also a system-level critique: groups, he continues, always take on a master (118); he has, he says, tried to function outside the ordinary laws that govern human aggregations — fidelity, competition and mastery — by what he calls 'the delegation of authority'. Only analytic discourse (as I point out below, Chapter 5) aims at meaning; it is because he considers it a radically different form of discourse that he can, starting from it, criticise the other discourses (of mastery, of the university, etc. (119)). And he distinguishes his effort from the limited political and economic one by drawing attention to the parallel drawn by his readers between his notion of the *plus-de-jouir* (surplus joy/also no more enjoyment) and Marx's surplus value: he claims his notion is 'much more radical'. His aim is to be able, in terms of his theory, to put the *objet a* in the place of the master signifier, the phallus. He felt great things hung on what amounted to a reorganisation of the rules by which we enter into the human group. The scope of the claims made by Lacan needs careful examination — an examination I begin in the next chapter. But I want to take one more example of the student who has moved from literary or linguistic analysis into treating patients.

Another linguist and literary critic who has recently moved into analytic practice is Julia Kristeva. What is perhaps instructive, however, about the route she has taken in relation to Lacan is that, since she has begun her practice, her writing has tended to become methodologically disconnected from Lacan. In *Powers of Horror*, she cites Freud, British anthropology, fiction, far more often than Lacan. Extracting from Lacan his 'conclusions' (about the remainder, abjection, the suppression of metonymy, the relation to the One), Kristeva arrives at what I have elsewhere shown[10] is a very different destination from Lacan, different because she thinks in terms of destinations, of ends, of finality. Lacan's effort was, I shall show, to avoid closure. Kristeva often engages in a silent and, I think, hostile dialogue with Lacan, that is, with his methods, his acute attention to the words his analysands use as a way of determining the meaning, the social link, they hide. In Kristeva's reports on her patients, we get occasional semantic references, but those usually to famous phrases from cases picked out by Freud. When we try to get a concrete picture of her 'case histories', we cannot. What we miss is the only thing we get in Lacan — *their* words. This is so because Kristeva, unlike Lacan, accepts the power and the necessity of the word; she subjects herself to *logos*:[11] Lacan never did.

Kristeva's vision is that we are caught inside the circle of language, which for her is what separates us from animal, biological life. But unlike Lacan, Kristeva never questions the absoluteness of the circle. For her it is a fixed boundary, one we can (if we are women, on the threshold between Nature and Culture) look nostalgically, longingly 'beyond' — across the limit of language, and towards 'the unsymbolised instinctual drives' which 'elude social intercourse' and the 'contract of desire' (*Desire in Language*, N.Y., Columbia University Press, 1980, 237–70). As a woman, she longs for a 'regressive extinction of symbolic capabilities'.

What Kristeva's stance amounts to is a giving up of the *critical* side of psychoanalysis, the side that criticises the word, culture, and the idea of the circle, *with the aim of modifying them*, or resisting their power. By her despair of being able to criticise she is perhaps all too easily acquiescing in the spread of her patients' illnesses. And because she does not practise her culture criticism by close attention to the words, the language in which culture makes itself heard, she has unduly restricted her options for making any major revisions of the *status quo*. But then, she does not really want to.

Her difference from Lacan is most acutely revealed perhaps in her sense that the 'division of the sexes is something much more archaic and fundamental then the one into languages' (D, 241); for her the 'biological and social programme of the species would be ciphered in confrontation with language, exposed to its influence, but independent from it' (241). The *symbolic* destiny of the speaking animal is superimposed for her over the *biological* destiny, which remains fundamental, a ground.

For Lacan, as I intend to show, it is precisely the division into sexes *in language* that is a process of rejection of the sexual *relation*. And division is, for Lacan, dependent on language, or more precisely, the symbol, since it can be accomplished through formulas expressed mathematically and in physics (splitting of the atom) (*4FC*, 204).

Literary Readings: Derrida Meets Lacan

Reading through Lacan to Derrida has, literarily, been fruitful: Barbara Johnson's succinct and justly renowned synthesis of Lacan's thought in her classic article on 'The Frame of Reference'[12] is enabled by her text's being the place where Lacan and Derrida meet. Using only the French *Ecrits* (which, however, contain some *séminaires*), Johnson is able to go beyond the formalist enthusiasm of her Yale mentor, Shoshana Felman, and to work simultaneously with the literary and the intersubjective aspects of Lacan's work. She 'gets' Lacan's meaning; prompted by her reading of Derrida, she neither celebrates nor formalises the signifier as that which has no meaning.

Johnson mentions Lacan's treatment of 'odd' and 'even' in his seminar (*II*, xv, 212 ff., 'Pair ou impair') that preceded the

one on the purloined letter. In this seminar, what Lacan points
to is Poe's treatment of the boy who always wins at odd-and-
even in the story: the boy explains that he is able to do so
because he imitates (Lacan calls it 'egomimie') the facial expression of the other player, and, once his face has so patterned
itself, he allows his mind to find the mental state that corresponds to this physiognomic set.

Lacan's response to such an explanation is to demystify it. We
are not, Lacan stresses, when we are in the realm of the numerical, ever strictly in the realm of the purely conceptual, the simple
unfolding of a series. Any unfolding or sequencing, any
temporal revelation, is already not just a cardinal series, but an
ordinal one — a path ahead, a diachronic order — and as such it
is based on values, on probabilities, not on sheer enumeration.
'What would be surprising would be to win or lose two times in a
row' (215); on one throw there is a 50% chance of winning on
each side, one only has a 25% chance of repeating his *coup*, his
success, the second time:

$$+\ +$$
$$-\ -$$
$$+\ -$$
$$-\ +$$

and on the third throw it is down to 12.5% that one will continue
to win or lose' (*II*, xv, 215).

We are, then, Lacan says, in the realm of symbolic signification: that of the 'plus-moins' and the 'moins-plus', not in the
realm of the real, where in a random series 'at each throw, you
have as many chances of winning or losing as on the previous
throw'. The coins tossed in the game are re-marked with a signifier of their value not as coins, but as 'odd' or 'even', the French
terms being 'pair' and 'impair'. And in this region of the
symbol, it is *two* that is the *odd* number. Johnson points out that
what Lacan is trying to think through here is not the eternal
(Oedipal) triangle, not the number One, but the number two
(469–72). But she does not offer us the reason why.[13] On the one
hand, Lacan re-emphasises the purely imaginary character of the
binary, dual relation once the symbolic holds sway. But on the
other, he evokes the idea that two might be thought outside the
confines of the symbolic.

31

Johnson misses one trick in Lacan's *Seminar on the Purloined Letter*, where we find the meaning of the 'two' Lacan is trying to rescue for the first time. Because Johnson is not attending to (nor could she on the basis of the *Ecrits* alone) the importance of the form of the social tie in Lacan, she overlooks the major question Lacan's text leads up to, asking of the hegemony of the signifier, a hegemony which he himself so amply illustrates: the question of the heterosexual relation. In the Poe story, it is the way in which the 'King' and the 'Queen' are *with* each other.

To get to that relation we need to return to Lacan. He has distinguished in the seminar between two 'registers'. (1) The first register is that of 'exactitude', of measurement, of accuracy. This register appears in the *compte rendu* of the affair given by the Prefect of the Police. His narrative depends, Lacan writes, on its exactitude being 'guaranteed' by his neutrality: he is merely a messenger, a means of 'linguistic transmission' (FE, 18). (2) The other register is that of 'truth', the narrative register which introduces Dupin with all manner of ambiguities, aporias and enigmas. This register is indeed, as Derrida complains, that of the 'truth' of the signifier, the truth of the phallus, the one by which Lacan writes, 'we measure the supremacy of the signifier in the subject' (FE, 20). It is where we are blinded to any criticism of the faithfulness of the witnessing in register number one. Here 'truth' is given a *gender*: it is a 'woman'. *A la* Heidegger, Lacan appears to be saying of Truth: 'Aren't we only refinding this secret into which she has always initiated her lovers, and from which they learn that it is on condition that she hide herself that she offers herself to them most *truly*' (FE, 21). But this 'woman' hides because she is 'castrated', because she does not exist except on the terms the signifier, which, as Lacan says elsewhere, while it appeals to the Other as the Truth even when it lies, ultimately prohibits all access to the *truth*. The woman, the phallic woman, the 'truth' is, in the register of the signifier, not there.

There is, however, *another* woman in the *Purloined Letter*: the Queen. And she appears to be anything but 'faithful', 'true'. She is also, as Queen, in a social position or role that is, clearly symbolic — in the 'merely symbolic' sense of the term — since she exercises, obviously, no ultimate power. She fears the King, and as such she is literally subject to him, to his power. Lacan writes,

Lettre d'amour ou lettre de conspiration, lettre délatrice ou lettre d'instruction, lettre sommatoire ou lettre de détresse, nous n'en pouvons retenir qu'une chose, c'est que la Reine ne saurait la porter à la connaissance de son seigneur et maître. (FE, 27)

[Love letter or letter of conspiracy, letter of denunciation or letter giving orders, subpoena or distress call, we can get only one thing out of this letter, it is that the Queen cannot, must not carry it to the knowledge of her lord and master.]

'Son seigneur et maître' — her Lord and Master. Not light words for Lacan, who analysed the discourse of mastery as one of the four discourses, the four forms of the social tie.[14]

The Queen is *really* subject neither to the signifier as such nor to the neutral code ('the way things are') but to the specific institution of marriage in which her husband is her 'Lord and Master'. As such, she has to play the game of the signifier, and bow down to it, not because, as Derrida suggests, Lacan thinks the *jeu* of the phallus is eternal (Lacan had a lot to say about the falseness of eternity) but very specifically because the Queen is subject to the moral order, an order in which a very concrete other — the King — has all the prestige, power and authority to make her keep her place. Barbara Johnson fails to notice this one thing, and thus falls subject to the 'truth' of the signifier.

Lacan, by this aside, this allusion, steps out of the circle made by the signifier, undoing, for a brief moment, its power to deal life and death, its ability to double and mask itself in the discourse of scientific, mathematical disinterestedness and neutrality (the Prefect). He exits by means of his barely audible reference to the *social tie* between the King and the Queen, her subjection to his will. It is this kind of move — this very move toward 'the social tie' — that I have been attentive to in Lacan's work. The preponderant weight is on the systems made by the signifier, to be sure, but I have sought for, and found, those spots where Lacan counters those systems. We have all too easily, like the brilliant reading by Barbara Johnson, in our criticism as well as in our lives, overlooked the social tie. Lacan wanted to demonstrate how willing we are to overlook it, to keep it offstage in our involvement with the signifier.

33

But he also, I think, wanted us to remember how disconnected we are.

Notes

1. From Lacan, *The Language of the Self: The Function of Language in Psychoanalysis*, tr. Anthony Wilden, N.Y., 1968, 49 (hereinafter *LS*). As I show in Part II, this 'wider' context is no less than that of the nuclear age.
2. See his recent book *The Ear of the Other*, tr. Avital Ronell, N.Y., Shocken Books, 1985.
3. I refer to his article, 'Le Facteur de la vérité', published in English in *Yale French Studies* 52, 1975, 31–113.
4. *Vies et légendes de Jacques Lacan*, Paris, Editions Bernard Grasset, 1981; in English, *The Lives and Legends of Jacques Lacan*, tr. Arthur Goldhammer, N.Y., Columbia University Press, 1983.
5. See articles by Laura Mulvey, cited below in Chapter 6 on the Symbolic Order. She stereotypes the role of the woman in psychoanalysis. On women see also Larisa Mykyta (see Intro., n. 2); Jeffrey Mehlman, 'The Suture of an Allusion', *Sub-stance*, 33/34, 1982, 99–110, who sees Lacan's critique of metaphor as an unconscious anti-Semitism, a resistance to the 'picking and choosing' of the Jewish merchant among others. See also note 11 below.
6. Paul de Man once told me that Sylvie Bataille, an actress, and former wife of Georges Bataille, was 'stolen' from the philosopher of the gift by Lacan. Clément reports she was a Jew. I know nothing of the historical accuracy of the gossip Prof. de Man shared with me.
7. *Jacques Lacan: Death of an Intellectual Hero*, Cambridge, Mass. and London, Harvard University Press, 1983.
8. Clearly he is on the side of 'castration', the castration that informs the imperative, 'Enjoy!' (*Jouis, XX*, vi, 13; see also Intro., note 17).
9. In the following chapter I demonstrate the cultural context of this 'renunciation of narcissism', but I also show that it is not through the agency of the superego.
10. In my 'Kristeva's Horror', *Semiotica* (forthcoming).
11. Centring her book on a certain kind of 'borderline patient' who relates directly to the Other because of his ambivalent relation to his mother, Kristeva attempts to trace the origins of Fascism, particularly anti-Semitism, to an abnormal, 'abject' response to the (for her necessary) Oedipal triangle. In 'Kristeva's Horror' I tried to demonstrate Kristeva's upholding of the Oedipal structure, and her equal hatred for its norm. I was particularly bothered by her attempt to pinpoint the Jewish Bible as *the* code that fostered abjection and therefore anti-Semitism. She finds that abjection is aboriginal in the person of the Jew because of his God, his emphasis on manhood, and the repression of the maternal, and that therefore he is the 'origin' of his own persecution,

since what he has 'repressed' returns to kill him: the death drive and the mother (*PH*, 112, 186). An extraordinary — and clearly motivated — extrapolation: Kristeva is working out something of her own, not Lacan's, here. For example, Lacan's work on the Jehovan phrase 'I am what I am' (above, Intro.) shows how its ambiguity offers a way out of the 'fallenness from being' that the 'good old god' (Mitchell, 140, 154) 'of all times', but particularly of Classical Greek thought (which Kristeva admires), gives as a self-definition to its subjects.

When she tries to see a positive side (which is to say, the side that resists) in culture her preference is for those figures who look beyond, but never disarrange, the circumscribed sphere of the speaking being, she is enthusiastic for Bellini's 'joyous' Madonnas who look toward, 'beyond', the circle, to the edge of repression. 'What makes the value of the icon', however, Lacan reminds us, 'is that the god it represents is also looking at it' (*4FC*, 113), and Kristeva's women do not disturb that relation. Kristeva veils the presence and power of the *tiers importun*, the Other, because she believes in it.

12. Barbara Johnson, 'The Frame of Reference: Poe, Lacan, Derrida', *Yale French Studies*, 55/56, 1977, 457–505.

13. Which is that the symbolic is the realm of unity and division-to-produce unity. Derrida criticised Lacan's 'triangles' because he felt they valorised Oedipus over the 'dual relationship which must be kept rigorously separate from the symbolic and triangular' (tr. B. Johnson, cited, 'Frame', 470): and indeed Lacan never ceased to remind his students of how the symbolic supersedes the binary relation. But for Lacan, the moment we are what he calls 'holophrased', that is, from the moment when speaking to the other centres the realm of negation, we are in the realm of the imaginary (the self-conscious) and therefore *en route* to the Other. He writes about the Fijian phrase 'Ma ni la pa ni pa ta pa', pronounced in a situation in which 'two persons are looking at each other hoping the other will do something which both parties desire but are unwilling to do' (*I*, xviii, 251). In this '*inter-regard*' each one 'awaits the other's decision in favour of something that must be done by two, but into which neither wants to enter' (251). This is not the primitive two-man origin of society for which Engels criticised Dühring; it is, he says, at the limit, the periphery of the symbolic (251). What Lacan is trying to bring out is that the idea we have of an 'intersubjective' relation (this is written in 1954, when intersubjectivity is in the air) is no less than an inter-objectal one, founded on a complementary natural satisfaction that clearly, in his Fijian example, does not exist; it is already ruled by negation, 'unwilling to do'.

14. The four discourses, according to Lacan are:

maître	université	hystérique	analyste
S1 ----) s2	s2 ------) a	\$ --------) s1	a -----)\$
------------	------------	-------------	-------------
\$(----a	s2(------\$	a(-------s2	S2(------s1
impossibilité	impuissance	impuissance	impossibilité

s1 = master signifier
s2 = le savoir
$ = le sujet
a = le plus-de-jouir

(*XX*, ii, 20: 19 Dec. 1972: 'À. Jakobson')

(Recall that '*a*' is the remainder (leftover, excrement, or what has been systematically 'left out'), the sexual relation; it is also a kind of surplus value, *plus-de-jouir* which is also no more joy.)

Part One
Lacan's Culture Criticism

Is not the maximum of light also the source of all obscurity?

(Lacan, *I*, xix, 263)

2

Word, Gift, Promise

Comparison is only a secondary development of the first emergence in being of the metaphoric relationship which is infinitely richer than everything I can outline for the moment. This emergence implies everything that can be attached to it later, and that I believed I had not said. By the fact alone that I formulated this relationship, it is I, my being, my admission, my invocation, which enters into the domain of the symbol. Implied in this formula is the fact that the sun warms me, the fact that it makes me live, and also that it is the centre of my gravitation (sun/heart) as well as its producing this half of shade of which Valéry speaks and which is also that which blinds and which gives to all this false evidence and tricking brightness.

(I, xix, 263)

Lacan's appeal to the student of literature lies in his emphasis on the cultural context of the inter-human situation: on the forms, not the meanings, of *how* we are with each other. It is easy, thus, to see the lines along which literary criticism has made the analogy between his version of analysis — his life-long effort to understand what the situation of analysis represents (two beings speaking to each other, their failure or their success) — and reading literature. Shoshana Felman, in a burst of early enthusiasm, writes:

The history of reading has accustomed us to the assumption — usually unquestioned — that reading is finding meaning, that interpretation — of whatever method — can dwell but on the meaningful. Lacan's analysis of the signifier opens up a radically new assumption, an assumption which is none the less nothing but an insightful logical and methodological consequence of Freud's discovery; that what *can* be read (and perhaps what *should* be read) is not just meaning, but the lack of meaning; that significance lies not just in consciousness, but specifically, in its disruption; that the signifier can be analysed in its effects without its signified being known; that

39

the lack of meaning — the discontinuity in conscious understanding — can and should be interpreted as such, without necessarily being transformed into meaning.

('On Reading Poetry', in Smith (ed.), *The Literary Freud*: Yale, 1980, 141)

Felman's breathless discovery (her second sentence is 11 lines long and consists of a series of four dependent clauses) of the lack of meaning, should however, itself be read carefully and more in the context of Lacan than of the Freud she has found through him. This enthusiasm for lack of meaning, for form, for the signifier, is indeed very important to Freud, to a Freud who wanted to believe in the myth of the civilising, mediating father (*Ornicar?* 1977, 7). It is also very Kantian: the form is the substance. What Felman does not see, in her insight here, is that form is *the* very question of Lacan. He fully understands the overwhelming importance of form to the human being, its ability to blot out and replace meaning — that which can only exist *between* two human beings — with significance, that is, with questions of *value*. But if he designates repeatedly the lack of meaning as the only meaning human beings have, does he also find it a cause for celebration? I think not.

Lacan knew perfectly well that the inter-human has lost its meaning — the unconditional demand of civilisation and culture is that meaning (which is, for Lacan, the inter-human recognition of mutuality) cede to form. For Lacan, the 'meaning' of the word — without the dimension of ambivalence — is the desire for recognition, before anything else there may be 'behind' or beyond the word (*I*, xix, 264). The inter-human is always given over to a medium which will shape and (re)direct it: language, culture. But Lacan also knew this to be the *source* of our ills, and his entire discourse, analytic discourse, is marked not only by a passive acceptance of the necessary suffering imposed by culture, but by a resistance to the sacrifice of meaning to cultural significance as well.

'In effect,' Lacan writes, 'a discourse such as analytic discourse aims at meaning' (Mitchell, 149, 'Une Lettre d'amour'), but, he continues, 'it is not saying too much to say that this meaning does not go very far':

What analytic discourse brings out is precisely the idea that

40

this meaning is mere semblance. If analytic discourse indicates this meaning to be sexual it can only do so by taking its limits into account.

If praxis, for Lacan, is 'a concerted human action, whatever it may be, which places man in a position to treat the real by the symbolic' (*4FC*, 6) then Lacan's criticism is not the abstract formalism of Felman's quotation. He is, after all, an analyst, a doctor, a healer. From the first work (his thesis on paranoia[1]) to the last, his anxiety is for the fate of the analytic situation, which is both a model of and a model for the *inter-human*. Lacan sees that circuit as a failure, as not working. Why?, he asks. What interferes and disrupts it?

For Lacan, the failure or success of the situation of analysis provides a model of/for that which is 'always at issue' in human life — the sexual question. Analytic discourse aims, Lacan writes, at a meaning, a meaning it knows to be 'sexual'. But Lacan writes that all analytic attempts to 'get at' this meaning are fruitless — even illegitimate — as long as the *forms* of sexuality have not been thoroughly investigated. What must be scrutinised are the ways in which 'sexuality' is apprehended, through which signifiers, and in what institutional shape. What is important here is that the stress on *form* is not a celebration of it, but merely a recognition of its preponderance in and domination of human life. What matters, for Lacan, is *how* you take form, your position or attitude toward it.

It is therefore ironic that students of literature who have become 'Lacanians' have often leapt away from analysing literature and into analysing patients: Stuart Schneiderman is one example; Kristeva is another. For literature is the place in which form is itself 'put on the couch', analysed rather than simply followed. The critical difference, for Lacan, will come between those who see form in the *general* sense, that is, who 'take things as they are arranged' (FE, 769) and those who take it in the universal (and moral) sense, as the ground, or foundation, of human things. It is this play between understanding culture as an 'arrangement' between human beings and culture as a legislating principle 'above and beyond' (which is somehow also 'below' them: *fundamentum* is *pudendum*; *4FC*, 5)[2] that situates Lacan's entire critical enterprise: For Lacan, morality is ideology as anamorphosis; both gender and the law of the law are what they are because their reality is unseen, hidden.

Sexuality and Civilisation

Lacan writes:

> It is certain that I came to analysis because I suspected that the relations between men and women played a determining role in the symptoms of human beings. That progressively pushed me towards those who had not succeeded in them, since one can certainly say that psychosis is a kind of failure in what concerns the accomplishment of what is called love.
>
> (*Scilicet*, 6/7, 1976, 16)

Freud too had noticed, of course, that everything that had to do with sex is a failure: 'Failure itself can be defined as that which is sexual in every act' (*Scilicet*, 6/7, 18).

The question Lacan raises is: Must the inter-human operate under the sign of sexuality? Is sexuality a universal moral law, or merely an arrangement? Lacan images forth the failures of sexuality in the specific form of the *word*. Although critics have been quick to believe that his intent is to show how grammatical arrangements, or categories, pre-position sexuality and determine it, grammatical rules are not, for Lacan, the material basis for the alienation of sexuality; but the *word* is. How is the word (*la parole*[3]) the cause (and the effect) of the disrupted sexuality? To answer this we need to examine very closely Lacan's insertion of the *word* into *culture*, particularly into culture as Freud saw it.

What Lacan does is to take the model of the word as that which is 'exchanged' between two speaking beings and show how the *forms* of what would appear to be a simple 'exchange of signals between two centres' is what determines and shapes their (sexual/social) tie: exchanged, the word is *given*. And it is only in the form of a gift, a deposit, or a promise that the word is 'received'. What is significant, therefore, in the form of the exchange is that what is given is not given only (or even) to the other: it is given to whatever it is that 'guarantees', validates or permits the exchange to occur at all. The significance of the gift is that, ultimately, it can only be given to this medium — to 'civilisation', to the law, to God — and not to the other.[4]

The Sacrificial Word: Gift and Promise

For Freud (1908), the difference between human and animal desire is taken for granted. Human, as opposed to animal desire, is directed immediately neither towards procreation nor complete satisfaction, but towards the gain of pleasure. And yet, we have managed to reshape this particular form of human sexuality in such a way as to give it principles, laws, including a pleasure principle. What Freud points out, in a 1908 essay on ' "Civilised" Sexual Morality and Modern Nervousness' (*Sexuality and the Psychology of Love*, Collier, 1963, 20–41, 27) is that it is the restriction of sexuality to the aims of *legitimate* reproduction that is the source of modern nervousness:

> It would be possible to distinguish three stages in cultural development in the sexual instinct: first, the stage in which the sexual impulse may be freely exercised in regard to aims which do not lead to procreation; a second stage, in which the whole of the sexual impulse is suppressed except that portion which subserves procreation; and a third stage, in which only *legitimate* procreation is allowed as a sexual aim. This third stage represents our current 'civilized' sexual morality. (emphasis in original)

The aim of the development of the sexual impulse within cultural boundaries is the 'union of the genitalia' (27) to which all aspects of the human cultural being are subjected and reorganised, from the pre-genital pleasures of the body of the infant, which must be brought under the hegemony of the genital ordering of pleasure, to the family, the pleasure of associating with whose members must be sacrificed to the demands of moving outside it for satisfying one's libidinal aims.

For Freud, then, civilisation demands the limitation of sexuality to heterosexuality for the purposes of reproduction, the union of sex-opposed persons to form another one. In addition (these are tantamount to the same thing), culture gains the surplus value of the excess libidinal energy that has been cut off by this limitation.

Desire diverted from immediate bodily and familial associations does the business of communal work: production and ultimately reproduction. The surplus of libido gained by culture has been considered so important for human life, Freud writes, that it has always been 'sacralised'. As a 'gift'. 'Offered to the divinity as a sacrifice', the 'communal benefit thus won was declared "holy" ' (*Civil.*, 25).

Lacan picks up these themes from Freud, and in reading them concretises and extends them in important and unexpected ways. It is not, as a kind of primitivist reading of Freud would imagine, so much the act of limiting sexuality and thereby producing heterosexuality that is the source of the proliferation of modern neurosis, Freud finds. Rather the source is a *supplementary* restriction in which the primary cultural law, the law of reproduction, is further restricted by another law, *the law of the law* of reproduction — legitimacy.

Lacan has asked what is the law of the law in this case? He answers that it is the Name-of-the-Father, the legal fiction of paternity instituted by modern, and particularly modern bourgeois, society. It is this fiction that, by supplementing the cultural reproductive imperative, strangles and subverts it, in effect precluding and preventing the actual practice of heterosexuality. The demand for 'two to make one' begins to hold sway over every aspect of the inter-human, so that unity becomes overvalued, metaphysicalised as an aim beyond reproduction and makes it so that, finally, there is only one sex, or as Lacan put it, only 'hommosexuality' (Mitchell, 155).[5]

The question of the Name-of-the-Father has received endless attention in Lacan criticism and I need not go over it here other than to contextualise it somewhat in the general cultural critique Lacan saw Freud as having made, and to show in what ways Lacan specifies Freud.

The second topic touched on by Freud here in this succinct formulation of the difficulties of civilised love has also been the topic both of Lacan's writing and more emphatically of what has been stressed by readers of Lacan: the sacrifice, or in other terms, castration. But it was not only as purely negative form, a 'cutting-off', deletion or castration, that Lacan conceived of the ritual sacrifice offered to human culture or civilisation. He focused also on the *positive* gift or offering. While anthropologists and sociologists (chiefly Mauss) had designated the unifying social function of the sacrificial gift in so-called primitive societies, it was Lacan's genius and his own particular task to distinguish the positive form of this sacrifice in specifically modern society. In primitive society, as critics have shown, what is exchanged is or has the value of the phallus.[6] In modern society what is most commonly *given* in our culture, Lacan finds, is the *word*: 'He gave his word'. (A word is not a word except in so far as someone believes in it: *I*, xix, 264.)

What would the word as a gift, as given — a promise — do in the terms Freud set? In what way is the word, that is, simultaneously a sacrifice of immediacy and a gain for culture?

It is obvious, of course, that the word (not yet in the form of a gift), like the image, replaces referentiality, presumably in the aim of communication with another speaking being. But it only produces the marvels of civilisation when it is 'given'. How?

The word, Lacan writes in his seminar on 'L'Ordre symbolique' (*I*, xviii), is devoted to ambiguity, it has no 'proper meaning'. Its function is to mask meaning. By hiding meaning (the inter-human) the word 'hollows out reality', makes a hole in it, and thereby opens the dialectic of truth and being. It is also that which, because it says what is *not*, can also introduce what *is*: being, as Benveniste showed — and Lacan was quick to point out — appears with the copula, 'is' and 'are' (see Lacan, *XX*, iii, 33, and xxiv, 40; and *III*, 340). Thus, the great irony of the word is that, by negating (the real) it introduces what is not, but does in the guise of what *is*. It creates the 'truth' of Being by the 'fiction' of the word. As such it will always fundamentally be devoted to this opposition (of truth and being) and to denying everything else.

For Lacan, it is only by means of the word that truth is hollowed out of the real (*I*, xviii, 254), there is no 'true' or 'false' before the word, because within the symbolic order, truth and falsity mean being responsible for, responding to, the word. Keeping one's faith, one's fidelity, one's promises.

The symbolic order becomes, as in Peirce, literally, the social order: the prototype of the other forms, imaginary and real.

For it is language itself that inflicts the mutilation, the wound, the amputation of desire — desire for the other, not as an indefinitely displaceable, substitutable pseudo-object that can never be an aim, but the other as a means of satisfying desire. It is by means of language that desire for the other is transformed into love of the Other, direction towards its particular enjoyment, its particular desire, the desire to perpetuate itself. (Far too much has been made of castration as merely a threat of genital denial, of genital denial as the foundation of culture, etc.; we need to see the positive effects, the marks and signifiers by which this threat is imaged.)

> Psychoanalysts showed that there were symptoms without any cause other than this: that the human is afflicted, if I may say so, with language. By means of language he supplements the incontrovertibility of the lack of sexual relations. What is social is always a wound.
>
> (*Scilicet* 6/7, 17)

The Universal Order

Everywhere Lacan finds that the *logos* is circular; what begins with language always comes back to language: 'Signification always relates back to another signification' (*I*, xix, 262). 'From the moment it is language we start from it is back to language we return' (*Scilicet* 6/7, 1976, 55). 'Things only signify within the symbolic order. The emergence of the symbol creates a new order of being in the relations between humans' (*I*, xix, 263). Even numbers take on significance, the value of the given word, in the seminar on the 'Purloined Letter'. 'Nothing makes sense until you put a sign on it' (*II*, xv, 215), not even the heart, the '*tumos*, centre de l'anthropos' (*Scilicet* 6/7, 1976): 'Only inside a symbolic world does a beating heart makes sense,' he writes, after stating that:

> Each time we are in the order of the word all that which installs in reality another reality, at the limit, only takes on its sense and its accent in function of this order itself. If emotion can be displaced, inverted, inhibited, if it is engaged in a dialectic, it is that it is taken in a symbolic order, from which the other orders, imaginary and real, take their place and are ordered.
>
> (*I*, xix, 263)

I think it is important to pay close attention to Lacan's nuance here. For his emphasis is not only on the symbolic sphere that makes up the discourse of human knowledge, but on its power to 'displace', 'invert', 'inhibit' human emotion, feeling (shaping it so much that it can even 'engage it in a dialectic') — *sentiment* or *sensibilité* in French, from the same root term, *sens*, as that of meaning. Although it would be easy to assume this is a Nietzchean demystification of sense as meaning by the use of sense as feeling, I think much more is going on here in Lacan. For 'feeling' and sentiment are not simply animal sensations, but are already linked to the inter-human, at least in Lacan's perspective. (See my discussion of 'Kant avec Sade', below.) Lacan's is rather, as in Freud (or Pascal), a dialectic between *sentiment* and *sens*, feeling and reason. Even Nietzche complained that the world needed to feel once again 'in the Kleistian manner', and found Stendhal (who wrote in *Le Rouge et le noir* that in modern civilisation, 'whenever a man of power meets a man of feeling he kills him') to be the greatest of modern psychologists. Power consists in the ability to restrict and limit meaning. It is the quashing of multiple meanings, not simply their elimination, that the hegemonic signifier operates. By imposing or implying 'significance' at the expense of meaning, the word becomes the basis of social life, the form of the social tie. It inverts or displaces feeling because, like the phallic veil, it never gives meaning any quarter, never allows it to be seen or heard in anything other than a 'significant' form. It does so with all the ambiguity that any gesture or tone has ever introduced into a 'clear-cut' meaning. Like the oracle, the word is the basic social contract because its form allows one to wriggle out of it: The word, Lacan writes, is devoted to ambiguity. As a signifier, the word refuses to restrict itself to meaning.

The word is instituted in the structure of a semantic world, that of language. The word never has only one use. Every word always has a beyond, sustains several functions, envelops several meanings. Behind what discourse says, there is what it means (wants to say), and behind what it wants to say there is another meaning, and this process will never be exhausted.

(*I*, xix, 267)

(A lot of Derrida is implicated in this 1954 quote.)

A word is not a word (*parole*, oath, vow are implied in this term), except in so far as someone believes it, takes you 'at your word'. It is the positive 'glue' of the social order, it bonds that order together. But to do so it must separate that order absolutely from feelings: one's word is a contract, a bond, a promise. Neither 'communication' nor mechanical trans-mission, the given word turns both speaker and listener towards the Other as guarantor of its significance, its value.

Let me give an example from Lacan's early *Seminars*, one in which he specifically discusses the situation of analysis in a way that both implicates and indicts the social order, founded on the 'word-promise'. In *I*, xviii, he lectures on Michael Balint, one of those immigrant Hungarian-Anglo hybrid analysts Lacan had occasion to criticise.

Lacan discusses several Balint cases in which the patient has a particular relationship to the *word*. One concerns a man who tells perfectly accurate, plausible stories about himself, but which, added together, are incompatible, mutually exclusive. The analysand is delighted when Balint finally calls a halt to his verbal over-narration because, now, he has found an analyst he can *trust*, who insists on his words being 'true' accounts.

The other concerns a young woman, a compulsive, nervous chatterer. She has tried many analysts, one of whom points out that her nervousness is part of her attempt to reproduce an infantile situation, an effort to get back to so-called 'primary love', to her childhood relation with her mother. While obviously correct, the analyst's insight is by no means curative for her, and she persists in searching for another analyst, ulti-mately selecting Balint. Balint, whose own theory of 'primary love' (the dualised mother−child relationship) should have found the first analyst's account correct, is, in fact, a better practitioner than his theory would allow him to be. Lacan shows how Balint begins to pay serious attention to *the word*.

Focusing on the forms in which the girl gives her words, Balint finds that she chatters so compulsively in order *not* to have to say something else. Balint probes, questions, presses her for what it is that she is not saying behind her verbal screen.

It turns out that the girl has a letter in her possession that will permit her to find a place of employment, and she admits that it is in fact this letter that has been disturbing her, even though as a letter of recommendation it is quite excellent, even calling her 'trustworthy'.

Lacan's commentary (257) is particularly instructive as to his own understanding of the link between the social and symbolic order and the situation of analysis. Without knowing it, Lacan writes, without theorising it, Balint has intervened on the symbolic level with his patient. How?

Lacan, circuitous as always, has been developing, throughout this particular seminar, the theme of the child. He speaks of how a child's word is often considered oracular, may even be idolised, but no matter how seriously it is taken, no child is ever considered bound by it (255). The situation of the child is that of Hegel's 'inter-human': the imaginary and passional relationship 'before' the master—slave organisation of the world into struggle and labour. A child's word, given, Lacan writes, 'before' entering the world of work, is not his *bond*.

What Balint has stumbled on — the girl's aversion to the term 'trustworthy' — is indeed a desire to reproduce the situation of childhood, but not the version of it as a situation of 'primary' mother love. It is instead that of the child as *not* engaged by his word, unlike the adult, who is 'enslaved' (Lacan's term) by it. The girl, in short, does not want to work, to be caught up in the symbolic and legal order. That letter, Lacan writes (the infamous letter that always arrives at a destination) is what would have permitted the girl to find a *place* — which is to say, become part of the symbolic organisation of human life: 'Le surgissement du symbole créé à la lettre un ordre d'être nouveau dans les rapports entre les hommes' (*I*, xix, 263): but this 'new order' never takes the form of the pure symbol, it takes the form of the word. The 'symbolic order' is only apprehended in the form of the social order and its division of labour.

Arrangements

The discourse of analysis, aimed at finding a meaning, a meaning that has been covered by the phallic veil of the promissory word, thus can only do so if it takes into account that the lived *experience* of the symbolic is as the social and the economic. This is particularly the case when we deal with sexuality. With sexuality, are we ever really in the supplemental realm of the law, the symbolic order, of the culture in which our sacrifice of sexuality is evaluated as a great gift? The lived form of the laws governing sexuality, taken as arrangements, neither foundational nor constitutive, show us only one thing about human, cultural sexuality: it is 'homosexual', there is no such thing as the 'heterosexuality' that culture promised as the 'new order' that would be created by the sacrifice of libido to it. Lacan writes:

> for everything having to do with the relations between men and women, what one calls the collectivity — nothing works

but

> Even though it doesn't work, it works, nevertheless, thanks to a certain number of conventions, interdicts, inhibitions which are the effect of language and are not to be taken except as of this material and in that register.
>
> (*XX*, iii, 34)

Much has been written on the subject of Lacan's reading of the division of the sexes, based on language, the signifier, etc., his most quoted example of the arbitrariness of the gender division being that of the boy and girl who arrive at the train station, the one finding they had arrived at 'ladies', the other at 'gentlemen'. Lacan uses this as an example of how the signifier represses the signified, barring the subject from the access to the meaning of the difference of the sexes, while at the same time giving them access to a particular place in the symbolic — but also the legal and social — order.

Critics usually avert their polite, civilised gaze from these lavatories, directing their attention immediately away from the actual institution (separate toilets) to Lacan's own attention to the *linguistic* marks of the categorical separation, 'Dames', 'Messieurs', to the signifiers and to the arbitrariness of gender distinctions that they create. I would like for a moment to move in the opposite direction, back to the concrete, to speak of how Lacan's example — separate toilets — can be read more richly if it remains a concrete institution, and how the general truth to be abducted from this institution — the separation of the sexes, the

the failures of heterosexuality — is much more serious and profound than any recognition of the simple 'arbitrariness' of
gender distinctions implies. Culture sorts people into sexes: that,
as Erving Goffman[7] has pointed out, is a pan-human cultural
arrangement. But the concrete institutions are derived not from
the initial generic arrangement (has any human being ever
appeared — at least until recently — as not belonging to a
gender?) but from the universalising, conceptualising, legiti-
mising and, ultimately, from the policing of these categories.

The mechanical action of sorting out and controlling sexual
borderlines is not the only thing that operates as a consequence
of this segregation, which after all finally assumes that a real sex
does lie beneath the artificial mask, and can actually be revealed,
if only at a later point in time. Lacan's interpretation of the
consequences of this simple act of covering the genitals in the
very place where people (especially the sexes) meet or come
together is much more disturbing.

The urinary laws of the segregation of the sexes create a situation wherein, as Goffman has written, except in the case of
mating adults, the mature genitalia of humans are not open to
cross-sexed display in public. Any apprehension of the 'sex' of
the other — in the strong French sense of the word sex, which
means not only the gender but very specifically the genitals —
that occurs in public, social life, depends absolutely on our
ability to make inferences about them. *Signifiers* carry the entire
burden of gender identification — the sorting out of boys and
girls: words, title, clothes, acoutrements. These are, barring the
actual *seeing* of the genitals, the 'essence' of the human, 'sexed'
being. As Lacan once wrote of Picasso's parakeet:

Picasso's parakeet loved his collar and sleeves: he loved the
essence of the man

(*XX*, i, 12)

To Lacan, this parakeet is like Descartes, for whom men were
clothes in promenade:

Pro-menade: Clothes — that promises *la menade*; take them
off and you have the *menade* [Bacchante]. To enjoy the body
when it has no clothes on leaves intact the question of what

51

makes the One, i.e. the question of identification. All love is like the parakeet, who identified with Picasso's clothing.

Lacan gives the example of Picasso's parakeet, the monk's habit ('the habit loves the monk, because through it they "are only one"') but any passage from Proust would serve as well. Picasso's parakeet loved the essence of the man, his clothes: the body under the clothes is left out, left over, *de trop*.

Lacan has discovered that *sexuality* exists *only* at the level of representation. Generic sorting precludes any direct apprehension of the genital act, the body: Lacan writes that we never know the body except as a form, or figure (*Scilicet* 6/7, 1976, 54):

> In order to give oneself an image of what is called the world, man conceives it as . . . unity of pure form, which represents for him the body. It is from the surface of the body that man took the idea of a privileged form. And his first apprehension of the world was the apprehension of his 'semblable'. Then this body, he saw it, he abstracted it, made a sphere out of it: *good* form.

Worse yet, we only love it when it is a good form: 'its appearance, men adore it' (54). 'Love' — this kind of love — the privileging and valuing ('good' form) of the subtraction or loss of the body is the form of the cultural compulsion to obey its ends. We must drape the genital act with a phallic, Oedipal veil. Since our apprehension of sex depends entirely upon what could be called 'metaphoric' inference, the replacement of reality with the image is the 'first' cultural act.

But whether it is called 'love' or tenderness, or any other mode of valuing *positively*, rather than *negatively*, the loss of the body, we are in another dimension yet of cultural commands. Goffman writes that gender itself as display is not yet an ideological form, 'genderism'.[8] For Lacan, the terminology is more philosophical: the image is itself replaced by the *concept* (translated in French as *figure*). Lacan writes, 'The concept is what makes it that the thing is there, while not being there' (*X*, xix, 267). (The concept is, Hegel writes, 'the time of the thing'. Only the unconscious knows no such conceptual time, that is, it is not under the hegemony of the concept or the figure in the sense that we are using it here. But that is another story, another scene.) As far as public order, modern culture is concerned, the function of the signifier is indeed to sort, to group and to polarise around the concept, which plays with presence and absence not in neutral terms, but in terms of *evaluation* (*III*, xxiii, 328).

Playing around with these signifiers is the occasion for high hilarity (*Some Like it Hot, Tootsie*): one laughs when their arbitrariness is revealed. At the end of Billy Wilder's *Some Like it Hot*, Jack Lemmon, in relief and anguish, 'reveals' that, under his dress, he is a man (Lemmon thereby assuming his millionaire 'boyfriend' will now reconsider his marriage proposal): Joe E. Brown responds, 'Nobody's perfect.' Lacan's insight seems to start somewhere more like this, the acceptance of a kind of mono- or non-sexuality as the truth of human sex, than at the end of *Tootsie*, in which the star's sex is securely 'known'.

The 'truth' of castration, the kind of truth that only exists within the metaphoric circle of the signifier, precludes, even in the act of 'revelation', the ability to 'see' the genitals: 'Nobody's perfect.' This is especially so, for Lacan, because of our model of perfection — the highest cultural Good in the form of a Supreme Good (Mitchell, 155). Human beings, he writes, confuse their own good with that which radiates from Supreme Being: the *filia* of the Supreme Good is, for us, misery (instinctual renunciation, sacrifice of libido). Whatever bond, or social tie, this model of perfection makes between human beings does so on the basis of their common unhappiness: Lacan calls it a fraternal bond: humans are 'brothers in misery' (Mitchell, 155).

But culture had promised that the bond would appear in quite another form: a bonding not of men, but of man and woman; not in misery, but in happiness. The monosexual, or, as he writes, *hommosexuel*, is the only 'love' relation that, formed by culture in opposition to the promise of heterosexual love, has ever yet existed.

—

The Reversal of the Message by the Code

Lacan seems to be haunted by the puzzle of how, precisely, the terms for order that beings give themselves reverse, turn back to oppress and deny them. It is the mechanism of *conceptualisation* — how and where desire becomes 'Love', work becomes 'Power', satisfaction becomes 'Joy', self becomes 'Ego', etc. — that concerns him, for it is in the concept that values are assigned to generic categories and, beyond them, 'pure forms'.

Rather than any one of these particular trajectories, I think it is important to start with the concept of code, the structural version of 'culture' and its difference from the *message*. These are the particular terms which recur (Lacan's 'structuralist' phase) in the *Ecrits*, and they are felicitous for his purposes of damaging the prestige (and the belief in our need to knuckle under to it) that we give to 'civilisation'.

On the one hand 'code', the 'pure' form. A simple opposition of presence and absence. On the other, the message sent in code from one speaking subject to another who can decode it, and reciprocally, return a response, made understandable by the commonality of the code to both.

But the transmission of messages is never a simple or symmetrical exchange; the mediation provided by the code interrupts as much as it facilitates communication. It delays or defers direct communication. If this is the 'good' side of the civilising principle (often the 'direct' form of communication is painful physical contact; a touch is not always tender), there is a 'bad' side to this mediation as well: it tends to do away with the message altogether: 'The speaking being spends its time speaking to no purpose' (Mitchell, 155). The code alienates as much as it familiarises.

Messages, that is, are always double-directed. As with the gift, the promise, the word, they are always as much addressed to an unknown, unmanned or unseen 'other' as to any co-present or known interlocutor. This 'Other' is witness to, guarantor of, their *value*: For the code always creates *value* through opposition, and only through opposition. Recall that, for Saussure, value is created 'in the absence of any external criterion'. Because the code is the locus of evaluation it demands involvement with it as more than just a neutral forming principle. The effect is that, because it interrupts the message from self to other, the actual absence of a response to his message appears to its sender as if it were an answer: the 'Other' provides the missing 'response'.

Intersubjective communication is where the emitter receives from the receiver his own message in inverted form ['où l'émetteur, vous disons-nous, reçoit du récepteur son propre message sous une forme inversée']

(Sém. sur 'La Lettre volée', FE, 41)

One gets, not an answer or response, but one's own message back in reverse.

What remains to be clarified is why the code is personified, why is it necessarily hidden in the guise of an 'Other' who can (or at least might) *respond*: why is it not a 'pure form' but a 'good form'? 'The Other is there to hide the code,' Lacan writes. The seemingly simple act of speech, the giving and exchanging of words, is ostensibly aimed at bringing self and other together. But it nevertheless inevitably drives them apart, or at least only brings them together in a *ménage à trois*. Speech itself, the given word, introduces this *tiers importun*.

Mechanically it does so because the grammatical code, the code in which messages are imbedded, is in part composed of persons: first, second, third. In the case of the first person, the *Ich*, the I, involves itself by becoming part of an *intersubjective* relationship to the code that governs speech. The 'I' is merely a signifier that designates a 'true' subject with which it can never coincide. Lacan lays out the exposition and the sentencing of this operation in the 'Mirror-Stage' and 'Aggressivity of the Ego' in the *Écrits*. The form of 'love' that governs this conceptualisation is *narcissism*.

In the case of the you, the mechanism of Otherness is the assignment of the copula: 'you are', or in Lacan's all too significant French 'tu es' — a pun on *tuer*, to kill. The 'you' is the impossible addressee of any message by the 'I': if the 'I' sees the 'you' as another centre, like itself, relating to it not as 'you' but as 'I', then it too has a hidden subjectivity, stands for that which is not. To say 'you are' brings in the dimension of the Other. The 'love' (or the concept) that gives the 'you' its law is *hate*: 'Because I love in you something more than you I mutilate you' (*4FC*, 263−75; also *III*, xxiv, 337 ff.).[9]

Benveniste has shown that the dialogue between an 'I' and a 'you' is the necessary precondition for the formation of a third person, he, she, it, they. But it is in the case of the he or she, that the crucial element in the 'life' of the Other resides. Lacan never stated this as such, but I believe he paid so much attention to the third person because it is the only one of the grammatical persons that is itself further specified, divided, by being *gendered*: feminine, masculine, neuter.

Ultimately, that gender distinction enables an oppositional and therefore hierarchical mode: 'he' is the positive, 'she' is the negative; 'he' is better than 'she'.

It also equally enables the denial and the masking of this hierarchy with a 'neutral', categorical, yet personified 'it' (also called the unconscious): a different voice of the Other. It is as the Other that culture, civilisation, will make its 'promises', its 'demands'. Even though, of course, these are only the return on/of our gift, our trust in it. The form of love that governs relations in the third person are those of brotherly, 'hommo-sexuel' love: *philia*.[10]

I must stress that, for Lacan, the Other does not pre-exist or pre-date language, there is no 'pre-discursive' reality. Discourse is everywhere coeval with 'humanity'. But the forms of discourse vary, and they vary as different ways of making 'social ties'. Only because language creates the fiction of culture as a closed, circular speech community composed of those who are 'in' on the same code, does it also call forth the concept of a Being exterior to this circle, the Other. If it did not insist on closing off (and clothing) that which 'founds' it (the inter-human, the genital sexual relation), perhaps the displacement of gender, its uneven evaluation — the price we pay for the word as gift — could be reformulated. But only if the 'love link' between them is also re-formed.

Notes

1. The 'erotomaniac' is someone who chooses as the object of obsessive love a more or less famous person, believing this person to be concerned with nothing but her or him (*Scilicet* 6/7, 1976, 10). In short, a person in love with a 'cultural figure'.

One of the first cases Lacan wrote about in his book on paranoia, *De la Psychose paranoïaque dans ses rapports avec la personnalité*, Paris, Seuil, 1975 (his 1932 thesis in medicine) deals with the erotomaniac woman named by Lacan, appropriately enough, 'Aimée'. ('Aimée', despite her liaisons with caddish men, her marriage and children, relates strongly to women — although her relationships are not actually homosexual — who eventually become in her mind imagined persecutors. One night she attempts to stab a famous actress, 'Madame Z.'.)

2. That is, morality is ideology; both are what they are because they are unseen, hidden, known only by hints — or by a 'bump' in that which veils them.

3. In the 'Seminar on the Purloined Letter' (FE, 18) Lacan distinguishes between the two words, *la parole* and *le mot* — the first, relating to the register of accuracy, exactitude and correctness has overtones of the sworn word; the second, apparently 'freer', liberated from relation to exactitude by the signifier, has overtones of the pun, the joke or wit: *mot d'esprit*.

4. If only, Lacan makes it clear, the 'love-link' did not have to go through words, if there were such a thing as the 'Symbolic' it could be *written* as a neutral, orderly formula:

$$x \quad R \quad y$$

in which x = man, y = woman, and R = the relation between them (*XX*, iii, 36). But to write this would be, Lacan says, 'une bêtise', foolishness, because there are no men and women, only signifiers of gender.

5. For Lacan, that 'the soul is conjured out of what is *hommosexuel* is perfectly legible from history' (Mitchell, 155). It is the relation to Supreme Being that fosters both narcissistic egoism *and* friendship, which he spells both *philia* and *filia*. That is because, if we see Being as an unmoved sphere from which we are excluded, then our desire is to join with it; when we cannot, we are, he writes, 'brothers in misery' — but a misery we think of as love and joy. For Lacan this relation excludes heterosexuality, or 'otherly love'. It is founded on narcissism, since 'the first being of which we are aware is our being, and everything which is for our own good will, by dint of that fact, be *jouissance* of the supreme Being . . . In short, in loving God we love ourselves' (Mitchell, 142). Lacan cites St Thomas as having had 'no difficulty in forging [this] out of [the] physical theory of love as it was called by Abbot Rousselot'.

6. See Anthony Wilden, *System and Structure*, on the implied parallel between the symbolic (economic) exchange of the Kula in the South Pacific and Lacan's symbol (255 ff., 268–9).

7. Erving Goffman, 'The Arrangement between the Sexes', *Theory and Society*, 1977.

8. Goffman calls the ideology of gender 'genderism'.

9. *III*, xxiv, 337 ff: Here Lacan shows the way 'you' is subject to the imperative mode of the signifier, is made into a subject, by the signifier. The *tu* is 'a punctuation point', in that it serves to identify, not a person, but 'the site of an order that is given'. It is promoted to subjectivity by the ascription of 'being' — the copula — to it. The 'tu' Lacan tells us is not to be confused with the *allocutaire*, i.e. one to whom he speaks, that

kind of 'you', subjected to the discourse (and master) of being, given a place in being, is killed: *tu es = tuer (tu es/* you are = to kill). See also *4FC*, 236–76.

    10. See note 5 above.

3

The Critique of Narcissism:
In Love with Culture

*The idea of the self as a body has weight, — it is what one calls the
ego. If the ego is said to be narcissistic, it is that, at a certain level,
something curtains the body as image.*

(Lacan, *Ornicar?* 11, 1977, 7)

Lacan repeatedly locates 'speech' as the origin of the alienation
(or expropriation) of desire by the community. Although it has
been explicated and re-explicated by critics, it is worth reviewing
here in the context of what I see as the radical nature of Lacan's
critique of culture. While it is true that, prior to Derrida's refine-
ments, too few made clear distinctions between language as a
symbolic system, or *grammar*, which is conceptual, and *speech*,
which is image-dependent, an appeal to the senses (at no matter
what level it is either eye or ear that is called on to carry the
message to the heart of the other), it is also true that Lacan was
partisan of neither of these aspects of language. It is reading that
is, for Lacan, the only 'intelligent' thing to do with language.

It is equally crucial to examine Lacan's attention to the point
where grammar and speech meet — in the speaking subject — in
the context of his resistance to culture, a culture viewed through
the critical lenses of Freud. Lacan always studied the 'I' and
culture as being in relationship to each other: in fact, he tried to
demonstrate that the relationship between the two has the
structure of an unhappy love affair.

The first being we love is ourself, as Aquinas knew. It is on
this first 'self-love' that we model our relationship to Supreme
Being, Supreme Good. By combining both the traditions (especially the French tradition) of the philosophical analysis of self-
love and the psychoanalytic insights into narcissism, Lacan felt
that he had forged a structural method for linking the individual
and the transindividual psyches.

It is customary, among Lacan's readers, to dwell on the

'structuralist' Lacan at the point where he traverses the phonematic code, phonetisation as governed by the play of oppositions between presence and absence, the paradigmatic pairing which constitutes the crucial distinction between phonemes (which can be abstractly conceptualised as positive and negative) with the Oedipal code. Seen as a play of presence or absence of the phallus, the negation of the real in favour of the possible, etc., the version of Oedipus known as 'the castration complex' founds the human being's access to civilisation through the process of identification. The ego, Lacan writes, is constituted by 'alienating identifications' (EE, 128). Identifying with what and, furthermore, why? The allure of identity, of identifying, stems, in Lacan, from the fact that the 'code', as a play of binary opposition $+/-$ does not arrange without also evaluating: presence is good, absence bad (or vice versa). What is quite literally absent from the code — the material body, for example — appears to be given either a positive or negative evaluation. In this way, what is merely an arrangement — here/gone, *fort/da* — comes to have the appearance of a 'foundation': a universal value.

A code presumably ought to be purely conceptual, neutral, a mere set of principles, of organising forms. Numbers, grammatical categories, generic classifications — this is the 'stuff' of the symbolic order, exemplified nowhere more efficiently and with more disinterested gracefulness than in the structure of language itself.

And yet, Lacan shows how the code is not only not disinterested, neutral — not even the numerical code remains so in his reading. It becomes a force, an effective process for actively shaping the interhuman when we personify it, which implies, ultimately, that for us, it is *gendered* (consciously or unconsciously).

Culture becomes an unconscious, a structure forming and shaping our lives. Like Freud, Lacan too tries to analyse the means by which culture alienates itself from 'civilisation', becoming a principle of negation and denial — the 'unconscious'. Not unlike Derrida (and in many ways, not unlike literature), Lacan uses culture's forms against themselves. First, linguistic form, and the way it identifies persons.

Persons

Culture as code gives itself to us in personal, subjective form: not merely a Symbolic Order, it takes on (necessarily so if it is to do its work) the guise of the Other. As Lacan puts it, 'The Other functions to conceal the Code' (EE, 233).

Culture is always experienced as an *intersubjective discourse*. In this process, the relationship of self to other is definitively cancelled in favour of what Lacan now calls the relation of subject to Other. And it is an amorous relation. In a kind of classic replay of Feuerbach and Marx, Lacan uses the *Ecrits* to disclose the mechanisms that operate the transformation of principle into person, and of the self into a subject, the mechanism, the narcissistic relation, that allows us to love our oppressor. The work is accomplished by the *image* (*imago* as determinant of the self, as the centre of an *Umwelt*, i.e. an ego) and by the *concept* (symbolic and ideal identification, especially gender identification). Culture is, in short, the product of the *sign* (image + concept). It is an 'inter-human' production. But culture's seemingly autonomous power, however, derives from something other than the *sign*: its energy source is the *splitting* of the sign through *metaphor*. Metaphor is, as Derrida once put it, 'irreducible' in language; it accompanies the originary violence of language.[1] But as he, following Lacan's analysis of the signifier as metaphor, also discovers, its obliterative powers constitute the only legibility, the only readability we have of the sign (which it cancels). Metaphor (that is, the signifying form) is the only 'translation' we have of inter-human meaning. But it is also that which has barred that meaning. It is the bar between the image and the concept.

The Narcissistic Mode of the Subject/Other Relationship

In his article on aggressivity (1948) and narcissism, Lacan does not use a properly linguistic mode for formulating the steps by which the self becomes a subject with an identity by means of its relationship to a symbolic code. The importance of the article lies both in the fact that it tells the story of the self's relationship to culture in a way that corroborates the linguistic story, but also that it tells it critically, as a means of contesting the wide-spread psychoanalytic assumption that the job of analysis is merely to 'moderate' the effects of narcissism, and to reinforce the ego against the demands made on it by the double call of the superego and the id. The analyst is supposed to 'hear' that the patient's 'appeal' addressed to the analyst 'carries a secret within itself. "Take upon yourself," the patient is telling us, "the evil that weighs me down, but if you remain smug, self-satisfied, unruffled as you are now, you won't be worthy of bearing it" ' (EE, 13). It is, of course, the duty of the analyst to be 'apathetic' in the face of the patient's *pathos* — at least, that is the theory up until Lacan.

It is the very fact that neither the other nor the Other responds or answers the appeal addressed to him/her/it, Lacan finds, that is the source equally of disease and of health in culture. On the one hand, the 'healthy' reaction to the lack of response from the Other is to reinforce the ego, to be able to bear the burden of solitude in the universe, to make it so that one can manage alone. (This is the God is dead paradigm.) On the other hand, the 'unhealthy' reaction would be to create a fictional respondent, to hear response where there is none. In Lacan's view, neither is 'healthy'. The analyst is not going to cure by being a kind of unresponsive Calvinist God, acting as his double, and presenting, as Lacan writes, 'our own virtues and merits by way of example', to the patient (EE, 14). Instead, Lacan finds that the analyst must bring the patient's agressivity into play (in a quite literal sense of the term), so that it begin the process of 'symbolic subduction', the negative transference.

Why is this the case? Lacan is pointing out that what is at stake for the patient is, indeed, the status of his ego, 'that nucleus given to consciousness but opaque to reflexion marked by all the ambiguities which, from self-satisfaction to "bad faith" structure the experience of the passions in the human subject' (EE, 15) and which is actually a mask for the subject created by his interested discourse with the code, subjectified as the Other.

The characteristic modes of the agency of the ego in dialogue (an evident contradiction in terms) are 'opposition, negation, ostentation and lying' (EE, 14). As modes, these all exhibit what the French tradition calls *amour-propre* or egotism. So although the patient expects our participation in his illness, he cannot really bear this participation: it would wound this *amour-propre* to be freed from disease by anyone other than himself, that is, by the agency of anyone or anything other than his ego. Trapped in his ego sphere, incapable of dialogue, he can only hear his own appeal for help returned to him in the form of his telling himself that he will be his own aid, his own salvation.

It is at this point, Lacan writes, that the analyst will do his work not by responding sympathetically, nor by failing to respond in such a way that a judgemental response is implied (the apathetic listener). He has to replace the mode of the voice and the ear with the image, becoming, as he puts it, a 'pure unruffled mirror'. Coupled with his description of the ego as 'opaque to reflexion', the use of the term 'mirror' cannot be overlooked. It is in the mirror that the ego is first born as an idea, and it is in the echo of the symbolic voice that it gains its identity: the analytic mirror must displace — 'subduce' — these 'archaic imagos'.

In a dramatisation that parallels closely those eighteenth-century texts that treat the 'origin' of this or that human phenomenon, Lacan now gives his version of the origin of the ego in the narcissistic relation. The mirror, held by the mother, proffers the developmentally half-formed and muscularly uncontrolled child with its first idea — in the rigorous visual sense — of itself as a stable unified appearance. But as it is only an 'idea' or an image, it is not yet personalised, anchored to a self identical to itself, and separated from others. The lack of personal identification accounts, Lacan finds, for the absolute 'transitivism' one observes in children after this point — a child hits another, and says he has been hit; he cries because another one does. The image of unity, and a unity that can be damaged, applies as much to anyone else and to oneself. Like Adam Smith's morality of sympathy (or Rousseau's 'pre-reflexive pity' in the savage) the child is, at this point both a self, and an *idea* of a self, applicable to any such self that might appear on his horizon. At this point, its *amour-propre* is not yet engaged.

Egoism, a kind of idea of the idea, or ideology of it, occurs as 'individuation', an abstraction from the notion of unity to the notion of indivisibility. Oneness. The means for this further escalation are formal means, means provided not by the visual but by the symbolic verbal code (this includes the numerical and, eventually, gender codes). The code organises and reshapes primary 'transitivism' so that now it works according to positive and negative pulsions, the positive mode of 'identification with' and the negative mode of 'opposition to' other selves.

This mini-version of the founding of civil society as the founding of the form of individuation, with its dialectic of dependence on the presence of others whom one opposes to found one's own identity and of the simultaneous desire for independence from them (Kant's fellows that one can neither bear nor bear to leave), can also be read in Rousseau and Marx. But for Lacan, of course, this is not all there is to the story.

For the term for order created by the symbolic dimension is such that it actually promotes the sense that only a subject could be ordering it, a subject who judges. The code becomes the Other. The code regulates and reforms the 'transitive' relation to the other by means of an opposition and identification that will always become a hierarchical relationship of superiority and inferiority.

The self cannot conceive of the symbolic order as a purely cardinal principle: its only model for self-conception has been that of the idea of itself as ego, a person. It can 'think' the code only as another person. The self, alienated from itself in the form of the ego idea, undergoes a further alienation in the form of the ego ideal, identity.

The linguistic code orders by means of persons, 'I', 'you', 'he/she/it'. But the 'I' is an ambiguity, simultaneously the locus of immense personalisation and identification, and a shifter, available for whoever takes up speech. Thus the identification the symbolic order offers the self is no answer, is no meaning at all. But it does provide the form by means of which the self is compelled to question its own identity: it creates the fiction of a subject hidden by the person, persona or mask, both for the speaker and for the code that had provided it. The Other is there, remember, to 'hide the code'. The 'I' can now ask the question of its own identity not of itself, but of the Other, conceived as an absolute I, the only one who can say, 'I am what I am' (see Intro., n. 6).

The subject asks: 'What am I there in that place?' (EE, 194): in other words, it asks the question not of its meaning, nor of its absolute being (since only the Other has absolute being), but of its *significance* in the eyes of, the judgement of, the Other. The Other responds by making further distinctions, distinctions that intimate, but never verify, the ego's significance: gender distinctions.

One of the most critical of the 'transitive' inter-human relations that the code must rule by its principles of selection is that relation of reproduction — procreative sexuality, the human means by which the code will reproduce itself. The sexes are identified and then sorted, selected, divided from and, according to this forming principle, opposed to each other. The presumption, from the point of view of the self, is that this division will result in their eventual combination, the heterosexual pair who will produce the child and re-found the cycle. But it is a presumption Lacan, like Freud, finds cannot be so easily made, from the point of view of the system.

Speech: Persons and Genders

If It speaks in the Other, whether or not the subject hears it with his ear, it is because it is there that the subject . . . anterior to the signified, finds its signifying place.

(EE, 285)

The 'transitivism' of primary narcissism can be modelled linguistically as an I/you relationship. As 'empty' persons or shifters, the positions 'I' and 'you' can be successively occupied by the same speaker. But once language is spoken, what is its purpose and object? Transitivism as the actual touching of the other has already ceded to something else the minute language comes into play: one only 'figuratively' touches the other, appeals by eye (image) or voice (sound) to the heart or soul of the other. And already this means difference or distance between the two.

It is possible to imagine a kind of 'first moment' of language-in-speech. At this point it would function as a mediator, as a bridge between the arbitrary division, I/you, so that it becomes a kind of common ground, a commonplace, a way for the two differentiated persons to 'meet' and agree on their common desire. But even the act (or pact) of 'agreement' on their common desire brings into play a thirdness, the notion that something else not only *is* between them (i.e. shared), but *comes* between them, divides them yet again here in the very spot where there ought to be coming together.

The *third person* is the conceptualisation — and the ironic inversion of — that which lies between the 'I' and the 'you'. It is no accident that only the third person is a gendered, and therefore definitely *identified* personal category. Here the shifting, the transitivism of the first two persons stops. This occurs as a result of the conceptualisation of 'I' as 'oneness'.

The relationship of the 'I' now modelled as oneness, or the singular, precludes any relationship to you, except as a means of again forming a third person. The 'I' as ego cannot dialogue with another except in the form of a person, who is thus never really other ('you') but only another 'I' created according to the same principle of singleness. Moreover, the second person is, in Lacan's perspective, made equally inaccessible by virtue of its use as a means of approaching the Other. Lacan writes that the third person is always a fiction, it does not really exist (see Intro., n. 6), it is only created by the link of 'I' and 'you'. But then, for Lacan, that is the definition of discourse, which determines the form of the social tie between an 'I' and a 'you'.

If it is only in the third person that *genders* are distinguished from each other, masculine/feminine persons appear there, it is also there that their presumed synthesis or sublation, the neuter person, appears: it. In the third person, all transitivity — the self's wild tendency to become the other, to reach the other — is definitively gone, replaced with an orderly series of categorically divided units whose relations are carefully ruled by conventional (generic, grammatical, legal) forms.

The 'I' finds its 'identity' here in the form not only of personalism, but gender identification. 'I' now relates to itself in the mirror of the third person: he or she, asking of this order in which it is now inserted: 'What am I?' The Other does not offer the 'I' its meaning as a sexed person, it responds indirectly and ambiguously, 'You are a man, and, possibly, not a man', since in the symbolic, as distinct from the real or natural order, anything is possible. But the symbolic order, if it does not mean, always signifies: ambiguity has a certain aura, as Lacan writes as he tries to explain the relationship between imaginary and symbolic:

> Qu'est-ce que le sens? l'équivoque n'est pas le sens —
> l'équivoque est fondamentale au symbolique, soit à ce dont se
> supporte l'inconscient telque je le structure. . . . Le sens est ce
> par quoi répond quelquechose qui est autre que le symbolique,
> qui est — pas moyen de le dire autrement — l'imaginaire.
> (*Ornicar?* 1975, 91)
> [What is meaning [sense]? The equivocal is not sense —
> equivocation is fundamental to the symbolic, to that on
> which the unconscious — such as I structure it, is supported.
> . . . Meaning is that by which something other than the
> symbolic responds, which is — no other way to say it —
> imaginary.]

The symbolic precludes both sense as sensation, and sense as meaning. This ambiguity allows the alternation negative/positive, the oppositional mode of value-creation which is fundamental to narcissistic egoism, to align one pole of this significance-making machine to the personal categories engendered in the third person. 'He' is positive, 'she' is negative: the story is an old one.

In sum, the organisation of culture as the dividing-up of a common task — if only the task of continuing a conversation — for the purpose of coming together, inverts at the conceptual level, to become division pure and simple, in the service of 'unity' or, finally, a principle of singleness.

The Role of the Signifier in the Alienation of Desire

Lacan's work, in the *Ecrits*, is to admonish psychoanalysis to read structure, the structure that is between subjects. Tackling the alienation of desire Lacan finds several structural moments in which the dispossession has, culturally, already taken place: in the division of genders in the drive towards 'procreation'; in the division of need in the drive towards 'love'. But mainly he reduces the drive to its minimal equation in the passion of the signifier to become the signified — of the image to become the concept. The signifier, the image, has a passion, an energy; it also passively, without resistance, undergoes its translation into the signified: 'By submitting to the mark of the signifier, the signifiable becomes through this passion, the signified' (EE, 284). For Lacan this is what creates the 'new dimension of the human condition' (EE, 284), that 'in man, through man, It speaks'. 'It' is the locus not of clear meanings but of ambiguity, not of sense (either bodily or mental) but of significance. 'It' evaluates, doing so by blotting out and cancelling meaning, especially the meaning of desire.

Lacan sees the moment of figuration, the imaginary moment, like the mirror stage, in which the body becomes an image of itself, etc., as the first step towards the conceptual and symbolic, which is the second stage of 'alienation'. In the structure of desire, Lacan sees the first satisfaction of needs (by the mother, or Nature, who always satisfies) as ceding to the the mutuality of shared desire. But this mutuality, existing perhaps only as an hypothesis, yields immediately, because of the individuated narcissistic notion of the two needed to share, to a monologic 'pseudo-dialogue' with the Other, the inverse model of the ego. The subject, now isolated within his own ego, 'gives up' or sends his desire to the system, and expects, in exchange, an increase — the same kind of surplus value communal work in the interhuman is supposed to yield: he demands the *love* seemingly promised by the system. Lacan writes that the Other always implies that 'procreation' and 'love' will be the reward for the sacrifice of desire.

But the Other does not respond. And in the place of the love demanded, gives nothing. Or rather it gives desire back in inverted form, as an image of love.

The renunciation of the satisfaction of desire can only be operated by a mystification such as 'love' offers, love as eros in the form of a drive toward unity. (Lacan is anxious, in his marginal asides, to imply that love need not operate under the sign of unity, a unity whose only disruption, in Freud's own account, occurs in the 'shape of Thanatos, the reduction to dust' (Mitchell, 138).) There is obviously an obscuring of the process of renouncing desire, renouncing connection with the other through the mediation of a shared agenda for a mythical connection to the Other. Divisions appear to stop at a certain point: the ego of the individual. This then is the source of aggression, for Lacan, since the unity and singleness, the lack of dependence of the individual, is only an ideological anamorphosis of any cultural being whose entire existence is shaped by communal interdependency. Aggression arises because the 'independent' ego ideal will always see itself as pitted against its fellows, or against the structure (culture, the communal situation) personified as yet another individual person, or Person. The way in which 'civilisation' will moderate the aggression implied in the concept of the ego is to mask or hide the subjective nature of the Other (its being an inverse mirror-image of the narcissistic ego ideal) not by revealing its charade of masking the code, not by baring the purely symbolic and ordinal nature of the order, but by a process of *impersonalisation*: the creation of the generically neutral (neutered, castrated) person, the *It*.

The Scandal of Oedipus

Oedipus is a patterned set of reversals, in which the threat of privation is turned into the promise of completeness, unity and fullness. As 'castrated' you give something up (the mother; but also the real organ, the penis) in exchange for a certain freedom from the organic, the necessaritarian. It is the freedom from nature that only culture could provide. But a purely abstract 'freedom' could hardly appeal, in the vocal/oral sense of the term, loudly enough for one to make this sacrifice. The appeal comes in the form of a promise of a future joy — plenitude — to be delivered by what Lacan calls the conceptually rather than actually combined forms of 'procreation and love'. These are in fact metaphoric versions of the metonymic, combinatory, relation, which they rewrite.

The scandal, as Freud well knew, and which Shoshana Felman has so succinctly pointed out in her Austinian studies of Don Juan,[2] is that the promise culture makes is never kept. The human forsakes the simple, combinatory (in structural terms, metonymic) mode, love *in* the familiar form, for the metaphorical promise of free and future combinations. But the promise is never kept. Once inside the space of metaphor, one is in the sack, in the world of presence and absence now formed into a deferral — for ever — of presence by means of a process that is endless (within the circle), of substituting one thing for another. These substitutions are 'free' in the sense that they are no longer linked to the natural, necessary order of biological reproduction, but they are nonetheless regulated by a principle; the principle, precisely, of *freedom*, which one is not free not to obey. On *must* substitute one thing for another. In metapsychological terms this is because the 'aim', the satisfaction or pleasure yield of the libido, is deferred absolutely, and the 'object', that which is the means to this pleasure, becomes an end in itself, but an 'end' which any object can serve.

What makes Lacan's vision of how Oedipus 'civilises' so distinctive is that he is concerned with what we might call post-Oedipal culture: a culture that no longer promises. As he writes in the essay on 'Kant avec Sade' (FE, 766): 'the eternal feminine no longer calls from on high'. In other words, we live in a condition in which the presumable 'appeal' of heterosexuality is no longer an operative force. The 'promise' of 'passion' is absent from modern life. Yet culture persists all the more effectively — it marches on dividing, disconnecting and making (pseudo-) unifications — but no longer in the familiar forms of love, family, sociability.

If the first alienation of the human fixes upon itself an image that alienates him from himself, producing 'the energy and the form on which the organisation of the passion he calls his ego are based' (EE, 18; the essay on 'Narcissism and Aggressivity'), Oedipus was supposed to be a medium of overcoming alienation. (Lacan calls Oepidus *un truchement culturel* — a cultural go-between or broker; how far from 'mediation' to trickery, from *truchement* to *truquage*?; FE, 98.) As a secondary shaping and a secondary (gender) idenfication (EE, 22) that modifies, moderates and restructures the 'first' passions it should undo the damage and division done by the image. Yet Lacan still sees Oedipus, for all its promise of heterosexuality through 'genital libido' (EE, 24) as a form of narcissistic 'love' (since it provides no real model of the other [sex]):

Genital libido operates as a supersession, indeed a blind supersession of the individual in favour of the species, and its sublimating effects in the Oedipal crisis lie at the origin of the whole process of cultural subordination of man. Nevertheless, one cannot stress too strongly the irreducible character of the narcissistic structure, and the ambiguity of a notion that tends to ignore the constancy of aggressive tension in all moral life that involves subjection to this structure . . .

(EE, 24)

In Oedipus civilisation makes its promises: 'love' is supposed to be the recompense offered for the division into genders, the separation of self from other according to a categorical principle. Eros is supposed to re-unite, that is, it is supposed to foster, through heterosexuality, procreation.

But it is an impossible blind alley in that respect. For on the one hand we still have the narcissistic mode of relationship, now idealised, or ideologised, in the form of a relation to the Other which is an inverted image of the self; and on the other, the model of egocentrism simply precludes any relation between the sexes. Oedipus becomes a pure myth in the service of a culture gone awry on the basis of its own 'principles', especially the principle of singleness, unity and indivisibility. The process of symbolisation and abstraction results in one final, summational imperative: 'Faire un', make two into one, and this imperative will rule every aspect of human life. 'Pleasure in being together' becomes duty, the imperative of marriage: 'two become one'.

Lacan writes, 'L'amour est-ce — comme le promeut la psychanalyse avec une audace d'autant plus incroyable que tout son expérience va contre, et qu'elle démontre le contraire — l'amour est-ce de faire un? L'Eros est-il tension vers l'Un?' (*XX*, i, 12). [Love is it — as psychoanalysis, with an audacity all the more incredible because all its experience runs counter to it, promotes it — is love really a 'making one'? Is *Eros* tension toward the One?]

The ideology of unity, of indivisibility is, of course, just that, an ideology. What is covered is a new division, that between one and nothing, according to the principles of negative and positive value. In the joining and union promised all those who submit to division, only a 'half' will masquerade as a 'one'. All the prestige, all the power, and all the satisfaction will be on the one side and none on the other. Whether this is in the form of gender division, or what we could call the division between labour and

71

desire, the conceptual drive redivides the first division and produces the exit from 'the inter-human'. The figurative appeal to the other becomes universalised first as appeal to the Other, and then as silent faith in It: 'Somewhere in the Other, It knows' (Mitchell 158; *XX*, vii, 81).

Altruism, otherness could never be extracted from this structure, Lacan writes; and in particular that form of relation to the other known as heterosexuality, 'otherly' love. It is no accident that Lacan moves from a discussion of the impossibility of altruism directly into his citation of La Rochefoucauld's maxim that marriage and sexual pleasure are incompatible. (The conduct books known as 'marriage manuals' which claim the contrary are probably proof of his point.) From La Rochefoucauld he moves to a discussion of medieval love, which, whether in the ecstatic or physical mode, aimed at the reabsorption of man's ego without alterity. Each had to be placed within the Other, reintegrating the physical with 'Universal Good', the ecstatic with union with the Other, 'without alterity' (EE, 24). Of course, the aim here, as in all structures based on a dream of unity, is defeated by the means, the quashing of alterity.

The subjection of the arrogant ego by an Ego that is precisely modelled on himself (centred, unified, single; what Lacan elsewhere calls the 'good old God of Aristotle', or 'unmoved being'; see Intro., n. 15) becomes the source of double aggression, the hostility towards the cultural supraindividual 'Good' that oppresses him, and against whose fellows whom he wishes to be free of. Thus the double alienation of the self in a drive towards the unification and centralisation of the image of the self destroys both heterosexuality and promotes aggression rather than 'civilisation'.

Benign mediator to some, the code, as *intersubjectivity*, becomes, in Lacan's perspective, itself the source of aggression, the very negation of 'civilisation'.

In speaking to the analysts Lacan is, after all, writing about the contemporary, with its display (the world wars) of the greatest brutality in the name of civilisation ever witnessed.

Notes

1. Derrida, *Of Grammatology*, Baltimore, Johns Hopkins University, 1967, p. 108.
2. Shoshana Felman, 'Le Scandale de la vérité: entre Oedipe et psychanalyse', *Etudes freudiennes*, 17–18, Oct. 1981, 61–78.

4

Lacan's Two Discourses:
The *Seminars* and the *Ecrits*

There is danger in public discourse, precisely in so far as it is addressed to those nearest.

(Lacan, *Four Fundamental Concepts*, 23)

The erasing of the borderlines between the psychoanalytic and the literary approaches to culture has left at least some literary critics uncomfortable, uncertain any longer as to their role, their method. Should we not, as some of my literary colleagues have wondered, just 'become' analysts? The question is a serious one, and one which I think Lacan answers in advance. But he only answers it through the particular *forms* of his speech, his writing. I turn now to examining those two forms: the series of addresses published as the *Ecrits* and the teaching *Seminars*, which are as yet only incompletely available in publication.

The Critique of the *Ecrits*

The *Seminars* constitute an unclassifiable genre. Although presented orally, their aim is to undermine their own discursive status in favour of leading the student not to *listen* to Lacan — indeed, in a way to resist listening to him — but instead to read, through him, the text of Freud. In them, Lacan teaches by example, showing his way of reading Freud, his own way of being a 'student'. By their circuitous but textually readable disorganisation of the ordinary lecture style they actively discourage the student from absorbing their language in the form of intersubjectivity known as speech. They are also aimed at the formation of a new generation of psychoanalysts, and, we shall see, of culture critics.

The *Ecrits*, on the other hand, were almost all originally given as 'speeches' — addresses to conventional meetings of psycho-analysts — and can be called discourses (they are often referred to as *discours*) in the special sense Lacan also gave this word. In them, Lacan is trying to get the ear of the psychoanalytic profession, is trying to persuade them to *listen* to him. Here the situation, the discursive situation, is that of someone outside the closed circle of a professional group. And once such a little sphere has been marked off, the 'logic of the sack and the cord', may as well be applied to it. Any closure or circle, as I mention above in my Introduction, should be imagined as a sack, with a *cul* on one end and its once open side now closed off by a string. Of course, he insists, one never asks oneself 'Who pulls the string?' Once one is excluded from a closed sphere or world, why not take on the role of the puller of the string, act as its 'God', or as the voice of its bad conscience? In terms of the psychoanalytic group, no use in acting out the open boundary between student and teacher: the group is a closed circle, especially to Lacan. So Lacan imitates 'the voice of the master'. Why not? since a master's voice is the only one we deem worthy of listening to.

And although it would be easy enough, as some of his students have done, to sentimentalise the situation of these discourses as Lacan's failed attempt to be accepted, to get 'in', it is more likely that he saw each of these addresses as an occasion to question the very existence of a closed circle, and to bring the profession to its senses on what was for him always the most urgent of issues: the *démarches* of 'civilisation' and its anti-civilised form: culture. Cultures, like the model of the ego he elaborated, are closed to each other and aggressively engaged in opposing each other.

So what appears under the sign 'Writings' is precisely that which is, discursively, devoted to the voice, to getting a hearing, to speech-making. (It is noteworthy that, in the French version of the *Ecrits*, many times longer than the English translation, Lacan included a seminar on the Purloined Letter, and that, of all the *Ecrits*, it is this one alone that provoked readings by students of literature, and by that brand of philosophy (Derrida's) devoted to effacing the borderlines between litera-ture and the philosophical profession.) They are also, though often extremely technical in nature, resistive to systematisation and conceptualisation. If one reads quickly through these texts which span several decades, for example, in search of a clear definition of what Lacan means by 'desire', the results, even though tabulated neatly by Lacan's son-in-law at the close of the American edition, are ambiguous, each pronouncement on desire sounding oracular and laden with significance, but without any meaning that could not be countered by another meaning offered elsewhere. On *can* read the (unconscious) structuring of desire in the *Ecrits*, but not its 'concept' as a universal definition.

In terms of *the conceptual* the *Ecrits* could be considered to be strategically anti-conceptual on several levels, not the lowest of which is their attack on the way Freud's key concepts have been subjected to a radical reversal, at the hands of the profession, of their meaning and their importance. Lacan reinterprets their normative reading.

'Civilisation'

One of the major, determinative concepts that Freud addressed, and which Lacan made the subject of the speeches in the *Ecrits*, is the role of civilisation. The term used by the Standard Edition of Freud to translate his *Kultur* is 'civilisation', and not its possible alternative, 'culture'. It certainly has impressively benign connotations: the implication of distinction not only between barbaric, wild, savage and orderly, law-governed human life, but, more importantly, between brutality in the animal sense and humanity, humaneness. Freud explicated the civilising power of the incest taboo — formulated and reformulated as the Oedipus crisis and the castration complex — and he never wavered in seeing it as absolutely crucial to the process of civilisation as humanity necessarily experiences it.

Most analysts see no real other course for human beings, and very little reason to desire any other condition. To see the symbolic order, the order of the code, or law, as harmonising and synthesising is to see its positive aspect. Oedipus 'normalises', brings us into the domain of norms; it identifies and sorts us into categories that allow us to transform what Freud calls 'the family, with its erotic roots' into rational substitutes for the family — opposing sexes — in which 'boy' and 'girl' stand in for, and have transferred to them, the love for the father and the mother. The son gives up the mother for 'the girl' from another family; the daughter gives up, first her mother in favour of her father, and then her father for the 'boy' from another family. There are sometimes hiccoughs in the way Oedipus works — homosexuality, perversions — but these can be doctored, accommodated, palliated by the 'cures' offered by psychoanalysis. The promise is that of 'the happy ending', the reward for the sacrifice of libidinal pleasure (a pleasure which Rousseau once termed the pleasure of sheer contiguity, or 'being with') that pre-cultural or pre-civilised and/or familial *eros* provides.

That this is only a *fable* of how Oedipus works (ideally, ought to work) that the psychoanalytic profession has been listening to is what Lacan tries to make them hear. Psychoanalysis, in particular in its practical, North American form, has been in the business, Lacan finds, not only of retelling this story, but of adapting human beings to the particular culture it has formed. It is a culture where there *is* no happy ending, and never will be, since more than individual instinctual renunciation is entailed in the process of civilisation. What is renounced is the association with others. (Obviously a Rousseauesque rather than a Hobbesian fiction.)

What Lacan knows has been lost in this translation of Freud into the (especially American) institution of psychoanalysis is his critique not so much of Oedipus but of the *Kultur* that it is now forming. Freud criticised the means (e.g. the laws) civilisation uses to achieve its aim of reproducing itself because they were effectively subverting those aims; Lacan criticises 'civilisation'[1] because the order that it has created has become an end in itself. Freud found that children as the bearers of the code of civilisation are no longer being produced, they are blighted by perverse passions even in the cradle, as they become the locus of the displacement and substitution of the combinatory relation — love — promised and denied by culture:

> The uninitiated can hardly believe how rarely normal potency is to be found in the men, and how often frigidity in the women, among those married couples living under the sway of our civilised sexual morality; what a degree of renunciation,

often for both partners, is associated with marriage. . . . I would further point out that such a marriage will increasingly affect the only child — or the limited number of children — which spring from it. On appearance it looks as if we then had an inherited condition to deal with, but closer inspection shows the effect of powerful infantile impressions. As a mother, the neurotic woman who is unsatisfied by her husband is over-tender and over-anxious in regard to her child, to whom she transfers her need for love, thus awakening in it sexual precocity. The bad relations between the parents then stimulate the emotional life of the child, and cause it to experience intensities of love, hate and jealousy while yet in its infancy. The strict training which tolerates no sort of expression of this precocious sexual state lends support to the forces of suppression, and the conflict at this age contains all the elements needed to cause lifelong neurosis.

(*Sexuality and the Psychology of Love*, 38)

For Lacan, analysts have worked on the problem of sexuality and neurosis only from the point of view of one of its manifestations, not its source. They have investigated the neurotic mother, and not the *absence of the love relation* in which her 'neurosis' originates. Their gaze has fallen on the mother and not on the father; or rather, the Father, who gives the laws which pervert the aims of civilisation. These are not the laws of 'heterosexuality', 'incest taboo', and so forth, but the *forms* in which these laws are given: the discursive forms of 'knowledge' and 'mastery'. In these forms of social tie, all the positive sexual knowledge is offered only to one sex, the male, and denied the other, the female. Lacan's insight is into the importance of the role of the 'Father': mothers are 'real', fathers are only conceptual; to be a 'father' is, literally, only a concept. The role of the mother inside the conceptual space dominated by the father, as opposed to her role in the real, is a 'neurotic' mode, a mode which is, for Lacan, merely symptomatic and a consequence of the (conceptual) law of the Father. This insight is a major one, but it is also an extrapolation from Freud if we read him with a culture-critical eye. The partisans of feminism, if not the profession of psychoanalysis, have on occasion expressed their gratitude to Lacan for this different emphasis. (Mitchell, 55 and 1–57).

It is no accident, then, that Lacan's readers have displayed some ambivalences in regard to his version of culture as the Symbolic Order, for it has these two faces: the mediating and tempering side, and the repressive, unconscious, purely formal, side. It is also no accident that the major opponents of the psychoanalytic version of culture have been feminists.[2]

Oedipus in practice is not symmetrical: the mother's features are cancelled absolutely by the castration crisis, never to be seen again; the daughter is never really given up to anyone outside the family by the father, who keeps her as 'daddy's little girl'. That this is so, Lacan finds, is because the role that Oedipus enables us to play is not what it promised, that of our becoming members of a *community*, outside the family, in which we would be offered, in exchange for familial *eros*, the pleasure of being with others, 'combining with' them, according to the law. Culture promises such 'combinatories': 'love', 'procreation' (EE, 195). Without these promises, would we devote our energies and defer our pleasures to 'civilisation'?

Desire: Alienation and Cultural Production

Ever since Rousseau's *Second Discourse*, the term 'culture' has meant divisions — of labour for the production of commodities ('comforts', 'ease'), of self from other for the production of communal gain — and it has meant therefore the interdependence of those thus divided. Inserting himself into the tradition of cultural criticism begun by Rousseau and extended by Hegel and Marx, Lacan recognises this structure, although he brings the question of the gender division of labour to the fore.

For Lacan, as for Rousseau, human experience is structured by the culture into which it is born far more than it is by the primary relation to whatever it is ('Nature' or the 'mother') that 'satisfies all needs' (EE, 286). I think it is very important to emphasise how strongly Lacan intends this structuring to be read, especially in the context of criticising the ironic perversion of its own aims, the criticism that Freud levelled at civilisation. For Lacan, culture is a system of arrangements in which immediate satisfaction of needs is doubly deferred, although the promise is of a satisfaction far more elaborate than that which is possible in any undifferentiated, simple relational form, as with nature or with the mother.

Culture can promise the satisfaction of all current and all future, all possible needs, because its power to do so comes from an *original division* of the *labour* involved in procuring the means to satisfaction. Culture can be seen (Rousseau saw it this way) as a basic *sharing* of the work necessary to satisfy a need for a supplemental level of living, one that goes beyond necessities. In an ever-escalating manner, Rousseau's *Second Discourse* recounted how we moved from the discovery of 'how' to provide one comfort after another into new 'needs'. We go from satisfied necessity to satisfied necessity. We once randomly learned, for example, how to shelter ourselves: shelter is now a 'necessity'.

The *Second Discourse* also demonstrated the communal gain made in progressing toward the satisfaction of a need, when the work required to fulfil it is undertaken in consort with others. It is the communalisation of work that opens the world of *desire*. It opens desire because the communalisation of work depends absolutely on an agreement, between those whose labour is thus organised, on exactly *what* the desired end is. Culture can satisfy needs in such a powerful and accelerating manner *only* if desire is *shared*. And in order for it to be shared it must be *communicated* between the parties who will labour to satisfy it. It is here that human *desire*, as distinct from the 'need' of the infant, the solitary, the isolated savage, or the animal, is born.

Need is transformed into specifically *human desire* by deferral. Deferral on two levels: one, something (the mother or cultural cooperation) must have already satisfied basic necessities, so that what Rousseau calls 'new needs' come into play: once 'hunger, lust and a few other bodily appetites' (Hume, *Discourse*) have lost their urgency by being fulfilled, desire *arises out of this fulfilment*, a new 'lack' or 'want' is installed in the midst of satisfaction. But this new lack or want, which Rousseau said could never have arisen directly from the savage's condition (his needs satisfied, he sleeps), can result from only one thing, from that which *enabled* the satisfying of those needs: *language* as intercourse between different beings. Only language can provide the structure for modelling a common, as opposed to a singular, unique, need. Only language could provide the means for *sharing* or dividing up the task of fulfilling what is agreed to be a common 'need'.

Needs that can be fulfilled only if the means for procuring their satisfaction are redistributed by labouring at them from different angles require that the desire of one person *be* also the desire of the other. As Hegel saw it, in a phrase Lacan is fond of quoting: 'The satisfaction of human desire is possible only when mediated by the desire and the labour of the other.' Thus human desire, mediated (given its means) by the (shared) desire and (divided) labour of the other implies a delay, an agreed-upon deferral of the moment of consummation, due to its requisite journey through the other.

This communalisation of desire through language is, at its simplest, the first 'alienation' of need into desire. Like the mirror stage, it is not yet conceptualised, not yet 'pernicious' or detrimental to the consumption of desire. At this point language, the language of gesture, of appeal for aid in a common enterprise (if only the consumption of sexual desire) is not yet symbolically ruled.

But a second alienation occurs. In Hegel, it is (in Lacan's version of the ideologising of the ego) the moment of *idealisation* that is necessary to turn animal into specifically *human* desire. This idealisation, in its most benign form, is a figurative reading of need as desire, anticipation of a future enjoyment not yet at hand. The simplest forms of 'love' can be seen here, as are the first inferences about 'similarity' between the self and the other. The self, Rousseau writes, after repeated observation of the other, assumes that his motivations are *like* his own. He puts himself in the other's place; substitutes for him in what can only be structurally called a *metaphoric* process.

Where the problem for civilisation appears is in the rigorous *conceptualisation* of similarity made on the basis of an original division, a division that loses its aim through the conceptual process. It is here that the deferral of satisfaction is made the permanent condition of all cultural production. One anticipates, but never achieves, satisfaction: the substitutability of self for other does not operate wildly but is programmed according to a negative and positive pulsion that turns this version of 'identification' with the other into a mere masking of the process of opposing oneself to someone else: be it 'us' against 'them' or 'we men' against 'you women', etc. Thus there will never be an actual coming together' since a radical (though hidden) negation is operating the fiction of unification, resemblance and similarity.

Rousseau locates the conceptual, symbolic moment in which the course of communal desire is definitively blocked, in the movement from the linguistic figure of commonality, metaphor (in his example, 'man', which is already, Paul de Man finds, a blind metaphor)[3] to the numerical and quantifiable figure. Where did it ever exist? For Rousseau, only in fiction, the fiction of a state *between* savagery and culture — the pastoral, whose festivals already contain the seeds of egoism which will empower the cultural expropriation, or misappropriation, of desire.

Lacan also finds a specifically metaphoric process at the root of the disruption of desire, which he calls, following Freud, its *Urverdrängung*, or primal repression (EE, 286). What happens, according to Lacan, in his essay on the 'Signification of the Phallus', is that demand takes the place of need in a process of deviation that creates *significance*, as distinct from communal *meaning*:

> [Signification] proceeds from a deviation of man's needs from the fact that he speaks, and in the sense that in so far as his needs are subjected to demand, they return to him alienated. . . . [through signification], the turning into signifying form itself, from the fact that it is from the locus of the Other that its message is emitted.
>
> (EE, 286)

Need, as Rousseau also knew, always tends to become 'demand', 'new needs'. It does so even *before* it becomes desire, since desire is seen, in Lacan, as that need which is 'unable to be articulated in demand'. The Other (culture) is organised by the evaluating principles of negativity and positivity. Any appeal to the Other will be, it must be emphasised, an appeal to an inverted version of one's own ego ideal. Lacan finds that the demand addressed to the Other is always only 'the demand for presence or absence' (EE, 286). The twisted structure of demand (the inverse of need; the address to the Other in the form not of a request but of a demand) literally 'constitutes the Other as already having been able to satisfy needs' (286), since the Other is the locus of the excess of need over satisfaction. Any satisfaction of a need would therefore be seen as counterproductive, as counterproduction itself, since the demand for presence or absence appears, according to the narcissism of its form, as a demand for love. Thus, any satisfaction of a need is negatively evaluated; inverted, in 'positive' form, it becomes the demand for love from the system. It is this structure that becomes the (obsessive) cultural blockage to the satisfaction of need: culture promises but never delivers. As Lacan puts it, 'Demand annuls the particularity of anything that could be given' since anything given would only be seen, within narcissism, as 'proof of love' (EE, 286). The scandal of culture, is therefore, that,

> the privilege of the Other thus outlines the radical form of the gift of that which the Other does not have, namely, its love.
>
> (EE, 286)

The ego, now a subject, and the Other become partners ('neither subjects of need nor objects of love, they stand in for the cause of desire'), in the 'subtraction' — not the repression — of *satisfaction* from the demand for love (287). In other words, desire, as we are seeing it here, is a kind of switchpoint that can go either way: it does the work of Oedipus, and deletes satisfaction of need in favour of the process of idealisation and sublimation as a way of powering the cultural machine. It can also be a means of wrangling satisfaction out of culture, overcoming the alienation and expropriation of shared desire. In short, desire can have an egoistic and metaphoric form, or it can have a metonymic one.

For Lacan, 'division is immanent in desire' (EE, 289) (whereas the cultural drive is towards unity), a difference or 'particularity that appears beyond demand' (286) within the structure of an unconditional demand for love. Lacan writes:

> For a long time now I have laid down with a certain *There is something of One* the first step of this undertaking. The *There is something of One* is not simple — to say the least. In psychoanalysis, or more precisely in the discourse of Freud, it is set forth in the concept of Eros, defined as a fusion making

one out of two, that is, of Eros seen as the gradual tendency to make one out of a vast multitude.

(Mitchell, 138)

That the drive towards unity powers the machinery of culture, its productivity, while denying satisfaction to those desires its productions were supposed to satisfy, appears in the form of *eros* and is, of course, for Lacan as well as for Freud, the tragic irony of civilisation from the point of view of the inter-human relation, which depends on open recognition of shared desire. (Lacan writes, 'A brief aside — when one is made into two, there is no going back on it. It can never revert to making one again, not even a new one. The *Aufhebung* is one of those sweet dreams of philosophy' (Mitchell, 156). The radical reversal, an apparent regression, but a regression to what has never really been, to a state of culture where desire is between, rather than coming between. . . . On the edges of Lacan, beyond Freud, we read dimly the figure 2. The trouble with the Other is that it has no Other; or, as Lacan puts it in the essay on Narcissism, if our culture recognised *both* a masculine and a feminine principle, engaged in festivals and rituals that provided 'saturations of the superego and the ego ideal' (EE, 27) in which communal work and its meaning were publicly acknowledged . . . perhaps arrangements would be different. But, for now, alienation prevails.)

With the supersession of culture, the inter-human relation (the relation of recognised interdependence and mutuality) need never occur in the only way it can happen, willy-nilly, by chance, not by arrangement. It need never exist again. Culture can take over the business of redefining desire according to principles, especially the principle of singleness, but also principles of value-creation, negative and positive polarisation, opposition and identity, renaming desire as 'love'.

For Hegel (he parallels absolutely the paradigm created by Rousseau's *Second Discourse*) the second alienation also occurs through conceptualisation: the original sharing of desire and labour now becomes a rigorous and rational one, according to a principle of selection and division. Desire is now divided from labour, and reorganised radically by placing all the communal LABOUR on one side of this division, and all the DESIRE —

84

embodied in one master-figure — on the other. The aim is now 'shared' only to the extent that it remains as a recognisable goal of the labour of the one and the desire of the other, outside and beyond the grasp of either alone: Lacan writes,

> If, in the conflict of Master and Slave, it is the recognition of man by man that is involved, it is also promulgated on a radical negation of natural values, whether expressed in the sterile tyranny of the Master or the productive tyranny of labour.
>
> (EE, 26)

Up to this point, the end-point of the recognition of mutuality that creates human desire, we are still within the inter-human, that is, the common recognition of the aim of a desire which still takes its energy from the person and the ego, its 'passions'. The summation of this desire, now alienated, is the Master in Hegel (in Rousseau's *Discourse* it takes the eventual form of one enormous mouth — the monarchy — which eats up all the products of labour). We have not yet arrived at the oneness towards which culture is driven, since division and difference is still necessary to productivity; we are not yet beyond the inter-human circuit, because, as we all know, the slave is also master of the Master, who depends on him for his recognition.

We leave the inter-human circuit when *recognition*, the *knowledge* of the aim of desire no longer supplies the energy, the will towards the power of production. What Freud showed us is that we have moved desire's productivity beyond the personal, and beyond the inter-human relation. 'It' desires. Lacan's insistence to the psychoanalytic profession in the *Ecrits* is radical: we must reintroduce the importance, the significance, of the Unconscious in general cultural, not unique individual, terms.

> It is a question of rediscovering in the laws that govern that other scene [*ein andere Schauplatz*], which Freud, on the subject of dreams, designates as being that of the unconscious, the effects that are discovered at the level of the chain of materially unstable elements that constitutes language: effects determined by the double play of combination and substitution in the signifier, according to the two aspects that generate

the signified, metonymy and metaphor; determining effects
for the institution of the subject.

(EE, 285)

If we are correct in our demonstration that Lacan sees the *drive*
in culture as being toward *unity* through a 'symbolic articula-
tion' to a pure, conceptual systematic order, then the 'independence' of the narcissistic position framed by the ego model here
will not permit desire to remain at a level that is recognisable in
inter-human (i.e. interdependent) terms. The inter-human must
be subsumed under a concept that unifies both persons, both
master and slave, both self and other. Even the Other, hiding the
code that drives toward unity, has too much alterity; a further
hiding, the obscuring of the cooperative nature of desire, is
necessary for unity to prevail. The Other becomes the It. It dis-
solves the ability to 'think two', and in the guise of a 'triangu-
larity' or triplicity, it moves inexorably towards the One. Two
become one: 'It speaks in the Other'.

Culture (cultivation, but also the cult, the set of beliefs) is the
overlay and production of civilisation. It is founded by a rejection of the necessity and unfreedom of the real order in favour
of the freedom and possibilities of a symbolic arrangement of
human things. What is rejected into the real is replaced by the
word, one's proper name is obliterated by metaphor, by a stand-
in for it, according to a code (EE, 156). But by following, in
effect, the same logic of renunciation — or negation — that
founded it, culture has become a second order of organisation,
one shaped by a process of selection, that demands negations
and exclusions to the extent that it obliterates and negates one
part of the neat quadrangle Oedipus once seemed to promise.
An opposition grows, an opposition formed around principles
of positivity and negativity, and it condemns one gender to being
shaped only by negative. As Hegel once put it, in the section 'On
Womankind in General' in the *Phenomenology of Spirit*: 'The
internal enemy and everlasting irony in the life of the community
is created through the suppression of what the community recognises as essential to it.' This code — and it is as 'code' that Lacan
sees the cultural form of civilisation in the *Ecrits* — organised
around negative and positive drives, is seen by Lacan as having
been shaped by the systematisation of *speech*.

Lacan and Culture

Lacan always maintained a rigorously double register when he involved himself with anything that could be considered cultural criticism. Speaking to the analytic profession from a distance after the International Association had cast him out, Lacan expressed his broadest cultural concerns (in his words, 'the transindividual') in the terms dearest to the circle of analysts, the language of the individual:

> The unconscious is the chapter of my history which is marked by a blank or occupied by a falsehood: it is the censored chapter. But the Truth can be found again; it is most often already written down elsewhere. That is to say:
> — in monuments: this is my body . . .
> — in archival documents also: these are my childhood memories . . .
> — in semantic evolution: this corresponds to the stock of words and acceptations of my own particular vocabulary . . .
> — in traditions as well, and not only in them but also in the legends which, in a heroicised form, transport my history;
> — and lastly, in the traces which are inevitably preserved by the distortions necessitated by the linking of the adulterated chapter to the chapters surrounding it, and whose meaning will be re-established by my exegesis.
>
> (*L of S*, 21)

Lacan's first 'way in' to a critique of culture is through his analysis of the ironically uncivilised behaviour it solicits: in the form of the ideologisation of the ego. The climax of egoism, of narcissistic love as aggression appears, for Lacan, in Hegel, who raises it to the level of ontology.

> Here the natural individual is regarded as nothingness, since the human subject is nothingness, in effect, before the absolute Master that is given him in death.
>
> (EE, 26)

I have already treated Lacan's critique of the Ego: the personal, identifying signifier that opens the way for the development of the Other as 'Superego' — itself in inverse form — that oppresses him. In this chapter I have tried to demonstrate Lacan's critique of culture when it is modelled on the narcissistic love relation by re-inserting him into a certain tradition of culture criticism (Rousseau, Hegel) that hopefully situates his work. He is neither desirous of the overthrow of civilisation nor its champion. It seems to me that Lacan, in his writing, is armed with psychoanalytic insights into the relation of ego to culture (they conflict absolutely, in the mode of 'love'). But he is also mindful of the instructive blindnesses of psychoanalysis, such as its desire to believe in the benign Father.

By maintaining his double register, speaking of individual and transindividual in the same breath and with the same words, Lacan brings the relationship of self to culture to a critical point, a crisis. After Lacan, Oedipus may be dead,[4] but it is necessary to be all the more vigilant in respect to culture, especially its drives. Lacan has laid bare the linguistic, grammatical mechanisms by which culture is 'founded' — the persons, the words, the sacrifices. He has also shown how it has operated its alienating identifications through the promise of happiness, a promise he, like so many others (Freud, Kant, Rousseau), demystified.

What is much more of a momentous question, and one which it is my feeling Lacan tried to answer, is how we 'moderns' demystified about ultimate Good, Happiness, etc., no longer believing in promises and guarantees of good faith, none the less continue to exist as cultural beings without resistance to its drives, which no longer take the form of imperatives that promise ultimate rewards.

Lacan writes that, in modern life, we no longer represent the superego and the ego ideal in public rituals, communally recognised events: we keep them *offstage*. But this does not prevent their principles from being operative forces:

> What we are faced with . . . is the increasing absence of all those saturations of the superego and ego ideal that are realised in all kinds of organic forms in traditional societies, forms that extend from the rituals of everyday intimacy to the periodical festivals in which the community manifests itself. We no longer know them except in their most obviously degraded aspects. Furthermore, in abolishing the cosmic

polarity of the male and the female principles, our society undergoes all the psychological effects proper to the modern phenomenon known as the 'battle between the sexes' — a vast community of such effects, at the limit between 'democratic' anarchy of the passions and their desperate levelling down by the 'great winged hornet' of narcissistic tyranny. It is clear that the promotion of the ego today culminates, in conformity with the utilitarian conception of man that reinforces it, in an ever more advanced realisation of man as individual, that is to say, in an isolation of the soul ever more akin to its original dereliction.

(EE, 27)

To analyse this structure Lacan needed much more than the kinds of rules and laws that universal grammars offer: normative laws. He needed to examine the way we *arrange* things, our terms for order, even in the absence of any openly 'subjective' framing for them. Rather than *grammar* he needed to go to *rhetoric* for his answers.

Notes

1. Lacan never advocated the overthrow of culture. See Clément, p. 155, on the distance between the '68 student rebels, shouting 'Knowledge is useless', and Lacan's attempt, at the Vincennes campus, to 'build a critical university':

Their prodigious lack of culture dumbfounded Lacan, who had spent most of his life defending 'literacy' among psychoanalysts and who now had to face the negation of all culture, the non-negotiable demand for the establishment of a non-culture.

2. See below, Chapter 6 on the Symbolic Order.
3. Paul de Man, *Allegories of Reading*, New Haven, Yale University Press, 1979, 'Metaphor'.
4. See my recent essay, 'Oedipus Wrecks: Lacan, Stendhal and the Narrative form of the Real', in *Lacan and Narration: The Psychoanalytic Difference in Narrative Theory*, ed. Robert Con Davis, Baltimore, John Hopkins University Press, 1984.

5

The 'Value' of Metaphor

Let us say that the domain of sexuality shows a natural functioning of signs. At this level they are not signifiers, for the nervous (illness) is a symptom, and according to the definition of the sign, something intended for someone. The signifier, being something quite different, represents a subject for another signifier.

(Lacan, *Four Fundamental Concepts*, 157)

By his discovery, Freud brought within the circle of science the boundary between the object and being that seemed to mark its outer limit. That this is the symptom and the prelude of a re-examination of the situation of man in the existent such as has been assumed up to the present by all our postulates of knowledge — don't be content, I beg of you, to write this off as another case of Heideggerianism, even prefixed by a neo- that adds nothing to the dustbin style in which currently, by the use of his ready-made mental jetsam, one excuses oneself from any real thought. If I speak of being and the letter, if I distinguish the other and the Other, it is because Freud shows me that they are the terms to which must be referred the effects of resistance and transference against which, in the twenty years I have engaged in what we all call after him the impossible practice of psychoanalysis, I have done unequal battle. . . . It is to prevent the field of which they are the inheritors from becoming barren, and for that reason to make it understood that if the symptom is a metaphor, it is not a metaphor to say so, any more than to say that man's desire is a metonymy. For the symptom is a metaphor whether one likes it or not, as desire is a metonymy, however funny people may find the idea.

(Lacan, 'Agency of the Letter in the Unconscious', EE, 175)

Metaphor and Culture

Human forms of organisation, from kinship to prestige hier-archies, require a mode of selection. Hegel knew this, as did Rousseau before him: metaphor is the first human form. It shapes the incest taboo: the positive prescriptions for whom one *may* touch already imply the negative proscriptions of those whom one may *not* touch. It shapes paternity: the notion of engendering, of, as Lacan puts it, 'être père' radically depends upon a metaphorisation process, of making an invisible link between the sexual and the reproductive acts. And reproduction ('making one') implies *death* (one is all that is left of two). It also becomes the model for 'love' as the idea of selection, choice, absolute preference, as well as the desire for union, unity (two become one; marriage as 'two becoming one'). It is the basis of identity, and of 'civilisation' as well, in so far as it commands the field in which humans must leave their proximal associates (e.g. immediate family members), must relinquish mere propinquity as the basis of association without selectivity, and which offers the sacrifice of these to an ethic of reproduction, not of the self but of culture.

Inheriting a long tradition in philosophy and literature, beginning perhaps with Vico in modern times, and moving through Rousseau to Lévi-Strauss and structuralism, Lacan 'discovers' the primacy of metaphor in the formation not only of language but of all human institutions.

What Lacan's contribution consists in, however, seems to me to be showing how the negative side of metaphor — its ability to distinguish and discard, cut off, select, etc. — becomes a *determinant* of the social ties (discursive forms) between human beings. It dominates the linguistic mode, and it does so in the service of culture. In short, it becomes ideology.

The metaphoric mode dominates culture, repressing the metonymic. But the repressed may return. The 'other' possible scene for being human, the combinatory mode in which self might be 'with' the other, haunts culturally organised man, is given voice in utopian thinking (Benjamin's proletariat as the unconscious of society, dreaming society before it 'was organised into classes';[1] in dreams of revolution (Stendhal's *Love*, in which a permanent state of revolution is the only political order — which is to say disorder — that would promote a real relation between the sexes),[2] and in Lacan, resistance to the moral order. Lacan writes,

Mais pour y revenir d'ici que trouve l'homme dans la métonymie, si ce doit être plus que le pouvoir de tourner les obstacles de la censure sociale? Cette forme qui donne son

champ à la vérité dans son oppression, ne manifeste-elle pas
quelque servitude inhérente à sa présentation?

(FE, 508)

[But to come back to our subject, what does man find in
metonymy if not the power to circumvent the obstacles of
social censure? Does not this form, which gives its field to
truth in its very oppression, manifest a certain servitude
inherent in its presentation?]

(EE, 158)

The psychotic cannot leave the family, or what one assumes is its
'metonymic, material and satisfying mode'. But Lacan is careful
to point out that this 'other scene' does not *really* exist, may
never yet have really existed except by fictional opposition to
something else: the symbolic order. The image the psychotic
carries in his heart of the family is the family of the stray, wild
and spontaneous 'natural' connection; but for human, cultured,
languaged beings, it has never yet *consciously*, historically,
existed.

The psychotic is held by an unconscious, not of *ignorance*, but
of knowledge of the power of the signifier, or metaphor, to
cancel, to 'kill'.

I have from the beginning, articulated carefully that the
unconscious has nothing to do with [the ignorance of what
goes on in the body] but with what one knows, though of an
entirely different nature; one knows things that relate to the
signifier.

(*Ornicar?* 11, 1977, 6)

But just because it is a psychotic who is the last, in our culture,
to dream of escaping from the death by reproduction that
Oedipus, culture, civilisation demands of him, does it necessarily mean that the dream should not be dreamt, that we should
be so driven to eliminate the only thing that gives us any latitude
('the power to circumvent the obstacles of social censure'), that
is, the double scene on which to play out the human drama, by
reducing it to a single field, the field of the Other? That is the
drive of metaphor, the reduction to oneness. . . .

Metaphor in the *Ecrits*

Having language in common affords the possibility that what is said can be used not only as a sign ('intended for someone') conveying a meaning, but to signify, to 'gloss' what is being said with a coating of value. As Lacan puts it, language can be used 'figuratively' or metaphorically, 'to signify something quite other than what it says' (EE, 155). In other words — and Lacan is very careful here to stress that he is not talking about the use of the linguistic capacity to hide one's thoughts — the metaphoric aspect of language allows it to point the word to something beyond its literal meaning and referent, to obliterate its primary function of connecting two humans in a common desire, and, at the same time, to convey the sense of the *value*, the significance, of what is being talked about:

> What the structure of the signifying chain discloses is the possibility I have, precisely in so far as I have this language in common with other subjects, that is to say in so far as it exists as a language, to use it in order to signify something quite other than what it says.
>
> (EE, 155)

For Lacan, all *uses* of the word are metaphoric: from the minute language begins to do work on behalf of culture rather than on behalf of 'meaning'. What is the distinction between signification and meaning in Lacan? Lacan says there is *only* one 'meaning, the desire for recognition' (*I*, xix, 264); any other use of language constitutes a metaphor:

> Comparison is only a secondary development of the first emergence in being of the metaphoric relationship which is infinitely richer than everything I can outline for the moment. This emergence implies everything that can be attached to it later, and that I believed I had not said. By the fact alone that I formulated this relationship, it is I, my being, my admission, my invocation, which enters into the domain of the symbol.
>
> (*I*, xix, 262)

The only way to retrieve 'meaning', he says, would be to add up all uses of the word. Take, for example, he writes, the word *main*. In French it signifies 'hand', the body part that is its referent. But the minute you have an image, he writes, you have already opened a hole in reality big enough to let elephants in. What rushes into the word *main* is the symbolic order, at least in its economic form. For *main* is used in a variety of other locutions, including such terms as *main d'oeuvre* (labour, labour's cost), *mainmise* (authority, power), *mainmorte* (the alienation of a vassal's properties if he remained childless). An entire cultural and economic scene is evoked by the array of uses of a term which is supposed merely to designate a part of the body. (For Lacan we never know the body except as a figure.) As for self-conscious uses of metaphor, in literature, for example, Lacan cites the formula, 'soleil de mon coeur' ('sun of my heart').

> Implied in this formula is the fact that the sun warms me, the fact that it makes me live, and also that it is the centre of my gravitation as well as its producing this half of shade of which Valéry speaks and which is also that which blinds and which gives it all this false evidence and tricking brightness.
>
> (*I*, xix, 263)

The signifier — that image that is supposed to point to or merely designate — is, in fact, incipient metaphor, the starting-point of a process of annihilation and evaluation (the annihilation of the natural, the proper; the elevation of the spirit, the value beyond) which culminates in the figure as metaphor.

This is because, Lacan finds, the signifier is a means neither of expressing nor of hiding thoughts (wishes or desires), but '*underlining them in words*' (EE, 262; my emphasis). The Russian Formalist, Mikhail Bakhtin, anticipating both Lacan's and Derrida's linking of the sun and metaphoric selection by some years, once put it this way:

> We seem to perceive the value of a thing together with its being as one of its qualities: we seem, for instance, to sense, along with its warmth and light the sun's value for us, as well. All the phenomena that surround us are similarly merged with value-judgements.[3]

As the extension and elaboration of the signifier, *metaphor* is the systematic form of *classifying* and imputing value, or significance. Lacan followed closely his friend Jakobson's classic modern definition of this trope: it is the trope of *selection* and *substitution*. It is in this capacity that metaphor implies *choice* — this, not that — and choice in turn implies value-judgement. Any substitution of one thing for another is, in other words, the *preferring* of that thing to the other: '[Metaphor arises] when one of the [images] has taken the place of the other in the signifying chain' (EE, 157).

In the structural, basically Jakobsonian, version, metaphor is the mechanism of selection, the institutional form of *negation*: the ability to choose depends on the ability to sort into categories, and therefore to be able to say, 'this, *not* that'. It is opposed, linguistically, according to Jakobson, by the counterpositional form of metonymy, which is the form of *combination*, rather than selection.

Anika Lemaire, in her *Jacques Lacan*, which has been used as the technical manual for Lacan's followers, diagrams (and it is her diagrams that have 'stood in' for a reading of Lacan on these topics) the structuralist version of metaphor as negation and selection that Lacan borrowed, abusing them slightly for his own purposes. (As a cautionary note: Lemaire's thesis accents the linguistic framing of Lacan's work, emphasising the Saussurean direction of his thought. But her exploration of the implications such linguistic involvement has for any realm outside a rigorously 'psychoanalytic' problematics is quite limited, since, as Lacan tried to show, psychoanalysis unwittingly tends to an ideological bias in favour of at least one crucial metaphor, the paternal one.) For Lemaire, the essential division of language is along the 'two great axes' (part I, ch. 2), which are, she writes, *selection and combination*, rather than, as in Saussure, synchronic and diachronic. These axes, then, correspond, as in Jakobson, to the forms of metaphor and metonymy which are simply the hallmarks of the system, neatly displayed by Lemaire in diagrammatic or tabular fashion at the opening and towards the close of her book. The paradigm is quite clear, selection is supported by the form of opposition, and is arrayed in a 'vertical' or 'hierarchical' pattern; combination is supported by simple contiguity, and is arrayed in a horizontal mode.

From this initial opposition, all other linguistic forms flow:

Selection	Combination
substitutions	context
associations	
paradigm	syntagm
oppositions	contrasts
similarity	contiguity
metaphor	metonymy
language (*langue*)	speech (*parole*)
	(Lemaire, 34)

To this schema she adds the following (200):

I.	1. condensation	II.	1. displacement
	2. metaphor		2. metonymy
	3. substitution		3. combination
	4. synchrony		4. diachrony

which she takes as a representation of Lacan's conversion of linguistic principles in the first, Jakobsonian, diagram into psychoanalytic terms.

The problem arises in Lemaire's (and this is common in literary structuralism, as well as in psychoanalytic or any other structuralism) gliding from selection, synchrony and metaphor on the one hand to metonymy, combination and diachrony on the other, without reconciling the several analogies Lacan makes between the notion of *desire*, and between metaphor and *symptom*.

Lemaire equivocates on precisely the point we need to clarify in order to understand the role of metonymy — and ultimately of desire — in Lacan. For in the first column of the first table above Lemaire has placed *substitution* and *association* as interchangeable terms on the side of metaphor. But, as we shall see, they are only interchangeable if the 'scene' in which the metaphor appears changes. For the metaphoric power of substitution is a mode of blanking out an association — at least at the conscious level: its mode of 'like this' forms association only on the basis of a prior negation: 'not like that'. In the metaphoric mode it is only on the basis of a preceding negation, a linguistic 'not', that 'similarity' can be conceived. Whoever can associate love and roses (as in the Burns and Barthes[4] examples) can do so only by dissociating hate and roses, and also, because they will have made a prior distinction between 'rose' and '*not* rose'. Only this law of non-coincidence between rose and all other entities, this principle of distinction and division, supports comparison — our familiar literary version of metaphor — of love as 'like' a rose.

Lemaire doesn't understand metonymy (but then who but Lacan has?) in its disruptive function, its active determination of the form of a social tie. (In the final analysis, she closes the system, something she would herself be loath to do, making the mistake of doing what she accused Laplanche of doing — that is, of looking to metaphor as an elementary signifier which 'fixes' the never-ending process of displacement.) The tendency in metaphor is towards closure, encircling, drawing boundaries. It drives the subject by means of an alienated form of desire that Lacan calls the 'rails of metonymy'. But it is a desire that only mimics the combinatory, linking modality of metonymy. It will always centre and exclude. Desire, alienated desire, models itself on metaphor and therefore is a symptom. But the second alienation of desire — its 'derailing' — depends on the resistance to metaphor.

Metaphor, then, is the mode of *distinction*, of pseudo-difference and pseudo-similarity based on negation. It is, ironically, a form which, based on negation and opposition, ideologically parades in the positive character of identity and unity. Metaphor as distinction is to be itself contrasted with a much more general notion of *difference*, rather than opposition, in which each neighbouring entity is simply different from the next.[5] It was Lacan's particular genius — his gendering of metaphor — that has brought metaphor to its current crisis, and has perhaps opened the way for beginning to understand the metonymic mode, something which no critic — including the technically oriented Lemaire and the socially informed Wilden — have thus far been able to do.

Metaphor and Ideology

> Desire is situated in dependence on demand — which, by
> being articulated by signifiers, leaves a metonymic remainder
> that runs under it, an element that is not determinate, which is
> a condition both absolute and unapprehensible, an element
> necessarily lacking, unsatisfied, impossible, misconstrued, an
> element that is called desire.
>
> (Lacan, Four Fundamental Concepts, 154)

For Lacan, metaphor is an impoverished mode dependent on a
lack of reality, of meaning. But it presents itself in the mode of
excess, of surplus value: it always signifies *more* than it says.
This surplus is fictitious, a cover-up for its essential negativity,
its barrenness. In short, it is ideological in its culture work,
extracting libidinal energy from the subject with the promise of
productivity, while this promise covers over the subject's negation, and 'death' through transcendence. But Lacan characterises as 'neurotic' those who do more than accept the death-
blow delivered by the idealisation of desire as demand, of ego as
Ideal:

> The ideal Father is a fantasy of the neurotic. Beyond the
> Mother, the real Other of demand, whose desire (that is, her
> desire) one wishes she would assuage, there stands out the
> image of a father who would close his eyes to desires. The true
> function of the Father, which is fundamentally to unite (and
> not set in opposition) a desire and the Law, is even more
> marked than revealed by this. The neurotic's wished-for
> Father is clearly the dead Father. But he is also a Father who
> can perfectly master his desire — and the same can be said of
> the subject.
>
> (EE, 321)

Modern civilisation is both subject to and the subject of just
such a neurotic fantasy. Its 'unconscious' is, in Lacan's writing,
that scene which is dominated by the metaphoric mode. Its other
names are 'culture' and more specifically our 'economy'. Its
'other scene', dominated by the metonymic mode, is the dream.
In these two unconscious sites, the alternative trope is decentred

and devalued: in *culture*, metonymic combination and connect-
edness are evaluated negatively as retrogressive. Metaphor binds
by blocking the connecting flow of (libidinal) energy. The
surplus thus saved is then available for doing cultural work, and
it is offered to civilisation as a sacrificial gift, that is, a surplus
value.

In the dream as it is dreamt in opposition to cultural restrictions, free flow dominates: displacement is Freud's term for
something like the combinatory mode. But the promiscuity of
the signifiers here, refusing all significance, actually act as the
censors in this site. Only condensation — the positive side of
metaphor, its power to produce 'resemblance' rather than negative distinctions — allows what is blocked or occulted by displacement (certain connections or associations) to be set into
relationships with each other. As a switchpoint, it facilitates
associations.

Metaphor is, then, for Lacan, the mode in which culture
makes its 'promises'. Using a line from Victor Hugo's 'Booz
endormi', Lacan writes that 'metaphor is placed at the precise
point where meaning is produced in non-meaning' (EE, 262).
But the 'meaning' that Lacan characterises as *the* word, wit,
esprit, spirit, is not meaning as *recognition of and agreement to
the desire of the other*. (We know from Freud what wit does with
desire: it empties all of its satisfactions *into* the word, forsaking
extra-verbal and uncivil congress with the purported addressee
of the joke.) It 'abolishes' the proper name in favour of a
'higher' aim, something more valuable, more prestigious: Booz,
in Hugo's line, 'dies' or has his proper name blotted out,
'annihilated' (EE, 157) by what metaphorically substitutes for
him (the profusion of the sheaves Booz had contributed to the
communal welfare — 'His sheaf was neither miserly nor spite-
ful'). But this death of the natural man is supposed to be com-
pensated: the promise is that this is

in order to rise again in what surrounds the figure of speech in
which he was annihilated . . . in the figure of the burgeoning
of fecundity . . . the promise that the old man will receive in
the sacred context of his accession to paternity.

(EE, 157–8)

Here Lacan touches on what will remain an essential theme for him — the suggestion that the two modes, metaphor and metonymy, are indeed silently, invisibly, but unarguably *gendered*.

For Lacan, the metonymic connection — and it is as connection that metonymy must be understood for Lacan — between what has been occulted or substituted for by metaphor and the rest of the signifying chain is still present (cf. his note 18 to 'The Agency of the Letter' on Saussure's anagrams; EE, 177) beneath the cancellation of the proper name, the primary object by the metaphoric code. (Derrida radicalises: *à la* Heidegger, only the erasure of the proper by metaphor has ever allowed it to be seen; he questions the eschatology of the proper. But Lacan is also right, for human culture *as we know it*.) In the *Ecrits* he suggests, in a variety of ways, the domination of metonymy by metaphor. Booz has been murdered by, cancelled by, metaphor, and at the same time preserved by it through his ability to reproduce himself by means of the metaphor of paternity. For Lacan, the real Other is the Mother (EE, 286), her real 'connectivity' satisfies, thereby giving metonymy a feminine definition, but also a 'bad name' from the point of view of the cultural drive, in which satisfaction must be eschewed. The metonymic mode will constitute for Lacan 'the other scene' of culture, once this has been totally reorganised and codified along metaphoric (paternal, masculine, phallic) lines.

With the values reversed, the metonymic, maternal and necessitarian mode dominant, the 'Other scene' is then that of metaphor. Indeed the unconscious belief that the metonymic mode might prevail, would prevail were we not metaphorically vigilant against it, is certainly a component of the metaphoric drive of culture. Why, if we were not selective, if we did not give up childish (or primitive) things, we'd never get anywhere. . . .

Which is true, and not true. Certainly the accession to the paternal function through metaphor, the substitutions of others for the original objects of desire, not only civilises, it normalises. For Lacan, there is a civilising, mediating function to the symbolic Father which is 'fundamentally to unite (and not set in opposition) a desire and the Law' (EE, 321).

But the perspective lens of universal harmony has never been able to focus on the self, for it necessarily implies the self's denial. For Lacan, those who cannot accept their own death, cancellation and *Aufhebung* (resurrection through metaphor) become psychotic: President Schreber tries to hang himself, though seemingly cured, when a psychiatrist mentions to him that his case has 'engendered' a whole new analytic practice (*III*, xxiii, 329); he cannot survive his annihilation at the hands of a paternal metaphorisation.

Metaphor and No Value

Value is marked in the very form of this spiral developing towards a centre.

(Lacan, *Four Fundamental Concepts*, 271)

Why is the subject (neurotically 'normal') so intent on responding to the call from on high, for keeping up his conversation with the 'divine interlocutor' even though its messages are always 'interrupted' (EE, 186), its expected 'connection' never quite made? Because the Other is the guarantor of value, personal, moral, economic.

But, Lacan has us ask, is that value not a sham,[6] a confusing ambiguity if we expect from it not just terms for arrangement, but universal (moral) law? The subject attempts to identify his *being* by his location in a particular scene, in a particular order, by 'putting himself in the place of the Other'.[7] But already an ironic dislocation and dispossession of the self is implied in this locution, which elsewhere Lacan calls the constitution of the ego through 'frustration' (*L of S*) and 'alienating identifications'.

If the symbolic order is in fact only a system of differential *values*, then it is not a 'civilisation', even a culture, but an *economy*. What the subject signifies in that system by virtue of his place in it remains unknown to him, even though he is certain that 'somewhere in the Other It knows' (Mitchell, 158; *XX*, vii, 81, 'quelque part dans l'autre, ça sait'). Here is the double bind of the subject: if he identifies entirely with the Other as the *positive* pole of value creation (the 'origin' of fecundity) by putting himself in His place, he is acquiescing to a process which is essentially that of an '*Aufhebung*'. Whatever prestige and elevation he acquires also simultaneously cancels him: the subject loses his 'self' which then becomes a negative value, a 'minus one', the site of castration and loss. This is of course the *jeu* of the phallus (which Lacan calls the mark of the *Aufhebung*) which must hide from the subject his essentially negative evaluation by the Symbolic Order: its subjection of the 'individual in favour of the species' as Freud put it, or as Lacan said, 'the cultural subordination of man'.

The pseudo-positivity and prestigious evaluation of the phallus hides this negative evaluation of the self by 'curtaining' the body, partitioning the self from the other:

> the bar [the demon of shame] strikes the *signified*, marking it as the bastard offspring of the signifying concatenation [such that] the subject designates his being only by barring everything he signifies.
>
> (EE, 288)

The 'everything he signifies' is, of course, that *from the point of view of the system*, the universal, he is *nothing*. And nothing (the subject) divided by Nothing (the Other) equals, according to a mathematical principle — infinity.

Perhaps more radically important than the potentially sentimental reading of the operations of the Symbolic is Lacan's treatment of The Other in this relationship. It is equally marked by 'shame'. It, too, hides the fact that the Other as Father, as 'origin', the original site of fecundity, is an inversion of the sterility, the solitariness, the 'oneness' to which the subject has been condemned (freely and by himself). The Other is the site of lack of satisfaction, the opposite of the Mother. 'The sender receives his message from the receiver in inverted form': his sacrifice has been to 'the black God' (*4FC*, 275).[8] The promise of fecundity brings death, negation and absolute separation from the Other. Lacan writes that the subject and the Other are equals in this 'shame', this veiling of their mutual nothingness: they are, he says,

> partners: neither subjects of need nor objects of love . . . they stand in for the cause of desire.
>
> (EE, 287)

Neither subject nor Other *is* the Mother; neither the site of satisfaction nor the scene of connection and combination. There is no sexuality here.

Which, Lacan notes, inspires the aggressivity of the narcissistically alienated, desiring subject: the 'constancy of aggressive tension in all moral life that involves subjection to this structure' (EE, 24). The subjection of the self to culture incites the dialectic of passivity and agressivity associated with the structure of the ego. It is this dialectic that runs the *drive*.

The illusion of reciprocity — that the voice will be answered with another voice, the gaze will be met by another's gaze — only not that of the 'other' (*autre*) but of the Other (*Autre*) is the term on which the sacrifice of the other is made. The Other is supposed to return the gift, faithfully, perhaps with interest. 'I sacrificed for you,' the speaking being tells culture, 'now I expect you to reward me with your love.' But the Other does not respond. It cannot. The Other is not the Mother, after all. He was only a metaphor, only the signifier and not the signified (which has, through shame, through prestige been hidden): a mere parade. (Lacan writes of the proximity etymologically of 'séparer' and 'se parer': to separate, divide, and to adorn oneself: *4FC*, 214.)

The Role of Metaphor in the Production of Ideology

The Symbolic Order is the cultural and economic Unconscious. The negative aspect of metaphor fathers the Other, who promises much and offers little in the combinatory mode — 'love', '*être père*', '*faire un*' (EE, 195) — since its drive is the prevention of natural, necessary (and sexually satisfying) combinations.

Always bearing in mind that it is the 'form of a social tie' that is at stake in any figure for Lacan, I would like at this point to review the extent to which metaphor is the discourse of production and reproduction for the human being according to Lacan.

Centring and excluding are features of the signifier (whose role is, as Lacan reminds us, to 'underline' or emphasise), of all representations, and of course of all ideological (re)productions.

We are so deeply within the space of metaphor that its categories, general arrangements, have literally become 'universal': they enclose a world, centre it, make a hole in the middle of it, and they exclude. In this 'universe' — which is only a closed 'world' of culture — we act within a *scene*, giving everything we do the quality of being staged. For? The Other. ANYTHING which is 'staged' or 'represented' is already a displacement: *a failure to represent something else*. The question is *what*?

If we agree that ideological representation is a screen and a blind for something, that it is a positive depiction of something in order NOT to see something *else* (barred by 'the demon of shame') we may not, however, agree on the *value* and *nature* of what has been excluded. For example, Marxists often believe that it is the material conditions of production and the economic conflict of classes that are being denied representation in ideological form. But seeing 'the political' as the unquestioned, as unquestionably, *the* 'excluded' is difficult to reconcile with the shape of *contemporary life*: consider that the burning ideological questions of our day are reduced to whether it is a president's *face* or his *facts* that have been 'made up' for a TV audience. Questions of material production and reproduction are being staged and dramatically centred, dashing our hopes that there is an easy out from the economy of signs. We can re-mark the values of 'authenticity' that are ideologically represented (in rather ironic form) in this debate, but what class or economic interests are being masked by this staging of values would be either too superficial or too profound an analysis to undertake with anything other than semiotic methods. And since it is the conditions of the production of images that are being dramatically centred, it is clear that we need to review our concept of the relationship of ideology and economy to the sign.

Derrida's term 'economimesis' is extraordinarily apt for current US politics, the actor-president, a national image constructed of Olympic medals and photo opportunities. We have moved quickly from a politics of verbal, generally symbolic, rhetoric to the iconic (metaphoric) in politics. One need rarely attend to *what* political leaders say or achieve, pictures do all the work of 'meaning', as when the gigantic television screen at the national Republican convention filled with the electronic face of Ronald Reagan literally looking down upon a miniscule Nancy.

She appeared at some points to be prostrating herself before a deity — in a real sense, of course, she is. And if the iconic, or the 'masculine-metaphoric' in this case, becomes the dominant or exclusive signifier in our world, it is clearly time to counter it with some different rhetorical forms. For such a metaphor legislates the monetary relationships in the US economy as well; it does not distort or 'reflect' them — the feminisation of poverty, it is called, or the 59½ cent wage differential, etc. Tropes perform work for existing social arrangements.

Economies

Signs as signifiers are economies if they are representations. Wherever you have the signifier you will already have had a little area marked off, a boundary drawn, a distinction made, a negation. Now, because they are so *marked off*, signs create *values*: that is, within their sphere they can *metaphorically* (which is to say *economically*) be *exchanged* for each other. Whoever can say 'tree' has already implied '*not* tree'; but they can now say '*like* a tree' as well. In his *Metaphysics of Morals* Kant drew this same picture of value-creation through endless metaphoric substitutions or exchange:

> In the realm of ends everything has either a value or a worth. What has a value has a substitute which can replace it as its equivalent; but whatever is, on the other hand, exalted above all values and thus lacks an equivalent, . . . has no mere relative value, that is, a price, but rather an inner worth, that is, dignity.[9]

In this Kant prefigured Saussure's description of the sign organisation of value. But Kant hated it, and called for 'an autonomous member of the realm of ends' to be kept — without equivalent — not only outside but 'beyond' the value space opened by the metaphoric sign: here it is 'human dignity'; elsewhere it is aesthetics which should be placed *outside* value determination, to *be* the value of all such values. (It must be remembered that with Kant the exchangeable signifier of value takes its origin from a prior negation of nature.)

But whoever attempts to re-mark or draw this second boundary around the values of the metaphoric exchange creates an *economy*, by opposing the universe of values constituted by these signs to that which 'ought' to be excluded from it. But this is a double exclusion:

1. of the greatest and most *sacred* of values (God, the sun, etc.) or ultimate 'worth' which becomes the very *frame* around representation, supplementing the first negation that founds the sign with a second boundary-marker, another 'not';

2. and of the most reviled of anti-values, that which cannot, must not, be represented at all. This is what must not be seen, what has indeed been exorcised by the negation that founds the first sign.

Together these two exclusions form the *ideological* dimension of all *economies*. And they are dialectically related to each other. Only the *sacred* operates as a positive condition for value relations within the economic sphere; the negated, which produced it, does not.

Take our *gender economy*.

The Economy of Gender

What founds our *gender economy* (division of the sexes and their mutual evaluation) is the exclusion of *the mother*, more specifically, her *body*, more precisely yet, her *genitals*. These cannot, must not be *seen*. Hegel wrote that a community can only found itself by blindness to that which supports it absolutely — the feminine, the mother. And for all his ambivalence, Freud basically agreed. But this does not make of the woman the Other of the economy of gender, its ruler or legislator. That is still, according to Lacan, the position of the Father, of Him. The feminine gender is that which is not symbolised, does not explicitly partake of the signs out of which the Symbolic Order is constructed. Nonetheless this Symbolic Order legislates that there be 'two' sexually identified units within the order, an economy which, like all economies, is based on a difference within which there is room for only one of the terms to be marked with a positive sign. This positivity is created by a 'not': feminine is that which is 'not' masculine. The feminine is, in terms of the Symbolic Order whose economy is ruled by the law of the

Father, that which is the 'marked' member of the oppositional couple, male/female.

Within this framework there is a grave, though hidden, consequence. There cannot be, and has never been, such a thing as heterosexuality. The couple is no couple at all, but merely a masculine gender and its negation. The masculine gender derives from its identification, by means of symbolic substitution or metaphorisation, with the 'god' that subtends the economy, (a community which is limited, i.e. is not coextensive with the entire human community). The feminine 'gender' has access to such identification only by indirection, obliquely and incompletely. The process of *identification* is and must remain purely imaginary, a mere metaphor, even for the masculine; its structure demands, therefore, that despite the equality of its constitutive single, individual units, the 'feminine' be that which is unimagined or unimaginable except through a simple reversal of the metaphors of the masculine: If men are strong, women are weak; if men like sex, women don't, etc. The couple masculine–feminine does not exist. What we have, structurally, is simply + masculine / − masculine masquerading as heterosexuality. Lacan was not too polite to name that 'couple' for what it is: *hommosexuel*. He said simply that sexual intercourse has never existed, because we do not have, at least not yet, heterosexuality.

The weakness of this imaginary sexual economy lies in its failure to reach the real, to recognise that which 'supports it absolutely': the mother, the feminine. Some have argued that we must give the feminine access to symbolic identification, we must metaphorise it to bring it onto the closed stage of our gender economy.

The Ideology of Gender

If the exclusion of the mother's body is the NEGATIVE basis of a sign economy of gender, it is *also* the distorted basis of the positive depiction of its sacred values. The *body* of the *mother* anamorphically takes form and is (mis)represented as the *spirit* of the *father*. It is only in this travestied (transvestite?) representation that she is allowed to shape the internal relations of the economy, i.e. its *hierarchies*. The positivity of masculine identity forms the categorical basis of the evaluation of each gender:

only one, however, is aligned with sacredness, power and prestige. The other can only be formed in opposition to it. To give this gender positive value is to act ideologically from the point of view of structure.

Thus Lacan writes that the highest 'evaluation' of Woman — framed with the ideology of Dantesque—Petrarchan love is useful to the gender economy because its function is to *reinforce* and reflect the masculine identity:

> Un regard, celui de Béatrice, soit trois fois rien, un battement de paupières et le déchet exquis qui en résulte: et voilà surgi de l'Autre que nous ne devons identifier qu'à sa jouissance à elle, celle que lui, Dante, ne peut satisfaire, puisque d'elle il ne peut avoir que ce regard, que cet objet, mais dont il nous énonce que Dieu la comble; c'est même de sa bouche à elle qu'il nous provoque à en recevoir l'assurance.
>
> (Lacan, *Télévision*, Paris, Seuil, 1974, p. 40)

[A glance, Beatrice's, may be three times nothing, a fluttering of the eyelids and the exquisite loss which results from it: and here the Other that we should identify only with her own joy has emerged, that joy that he, Dante, cannot satisfy, since from her he can have only this glance, this object, but through which he announces that God satisfies her; it is even from her own mouth that he provokes us to have her assure us of it.]

For Lacan, the love of 'man' for 'woman' is not, historically, poetically or otherwise, for *the* or *a* woman in her particularity and as a member of the class 'feminine', but for her *generality*, for her gender, or more precisely for what her 'gender' reinforces in his gender. As a 'gender' she can be the complementary 'one' to his own oneness: and for that reason 'woman' as generality — and this is the major, the massive irony — is only seen in pieces (in part-objects, in the 'trash can' of overvalued zones of her body — breast, eyebrow, ankle, smile): any part that can be 'phallicised' or made, as a single part, into a metaphor for a wholeness that the woman lacks. It is, as Lacan and Kristeva point out, a love of abjection. What is 'loved' is the remainder, that which has been expelled from value in the metaphoric economy of signifiers: but not for what it — the *petit objet a* — *means* (the relation of self to other, metonymy, and

the sexual relation expelled from the psyche), but only what it is
allowed to *signify*: the Other. The gaze, the voice, are not from
the 'other', they are *objets a* which appear to come from the
Other: they fall from Being. They appear on radio, the television, the cinema . . .

The narcissism of the man which supports his ego and re-
assures him of his wholeness, cannot redirect itself as a love of
the woman. The Woman is, in fact, competing with the man's
own imaginary self-identification, and since she has suffered an
'amputation' she must inevitably lose by comparison with his
'wholeness'. Hence the failure of heterosexuality in the
Lacanian model.

How We Live within the Framework of Ideologised Metaphors

It is of course true that psychoanalytic theory is only an illustration of the metaphoric model of ideology, but it is the most
important contemporary one, since it proposes that the
Verneinung that opens our modern era is so much that of the
mother. Once we are aware of it, however, how do we act? Can
consciousness undo the ideologisation of metaphor? Julia
Kristeva, in *Powers of Horror* (and elsewhere) has tried to give a
positive identification, a sign or a mark, to the excluded mother.
She represents her as the pagan mother, or Freud's Minoan-
Mycenaean mother, full-bodied, joyous, satisfying, as opposed
to the phallic, denying Father who stages her. But in our model
such a positive depiction would have to be an *anamorphic* distortion of something NOT SEEN, decisively not itself given a
sign, for it to be ideologically centred. Perhaps the body of the
mother hides her head. Kristeva's may be an attempt by a very
intellectual woman to negate or exorcise her mind.

Now if we cannot simply counter one metaphor with another
to get *out* of ideological determination, how do we live with it?

There seem to be three current options or programmes that I
shall sketch out here.

There are those persons who, by opposing signs (and by extension semiotics) become the greatest supporters of the current
ideology that signs alone create.

There are those whose *stance* is a perpetual obeisance to their
own sacred metaphors, a continuous, if silent, evocation of their
'god'. Watch here for the (silent) trope of apostrophe, the

invocation, by intonation of sacred values as guarantor of one's own (economic) values. Here one speaks 'in the name of' sacred values (of 'the *best* that's known and thought in the world' of the 'finest of universities', etc.) in order to attack the 'levelling' quality of semiotics and critical thinking. *But* without, of course, *naming* the values, for names are signs and as such they have equivalents, i.e. are not 'sacred'. Persons who speak thus are the greatest obeyers of the sign, since it alone can create value hierarchies and distinctions. They cannot pronounce its sacred name.

Provisional conclusion: One way of living with ideologised metaphor is to uphold its sacred values in silence, by identification.

Those aligned with culture's values are most interesting when they are also victims of their ideology, when, that is, they can never themselves claim complete identification with the most sacred of values. I recently had occasion to review Helen Gardner's Charles Eliot Norton lectures at Harvard in 1979,[10] which Dame Helen took as an occasion to blast Frank Kermode's and Stanley Fish's treasonable smuggling of French goods into English language territory. She is particularly rough with Kermode's use of semiotics and narratology 'in the name of' her (in this case literally sacred) values, i.e. the Biblical structuring of narrative figures. Dame Helen was once well known for her championing of the new, her patronage of Eliot, etc. As Distinguished Professor at what may be the finest university in the world, Oxford, and a noblewoman, Dame Helen dismisses Fish's analysis of John Donne in a way that demonstrates my point. She finds that, after all, Fish fails to understand that Donne reads texts 'not to reveal some particular doctrine but the revelation contained in the word of God' (97) — a revelation to which the apparently agnostic Fish is deaf and blind.

There is more, for not only does Dame Helen want, in reading, to encounter God, she also reads to 'meet . . . the man' (84) behind the text, and outside *its* sign economy. She even describes literary life as a 'commerce' between great men (not seeing how this excludes her, of course), but more importantly this 'commerce' is the ideological support of what she calls the English 'birthright' (45):

Beyond our gain as individuals, the dissemination of know-ledge and the understanding of the past through its literature is a prime source of its own identity and cohesion, something very precious without which it can become a mere ant-heap or beehive devoted to the increase of the Gross National Product. This sense of national identity is not [watch that 'not': JFM] to be confused with a crude nationalism, or desire for national aggrandisement, or contempt for other nations. [*Of course it is*: JFM.] It is a sense of certain values, charac-teristic attitudes, on which our sense of community and of belonging depends.

She goes on to cite the case of England's resistance to 'the des-potism of Napoleon' by its recourse to those 'who spoke the tongue of Shakespeare':

In happier times there works almost unconsciously and subtly a sense of certain long-established virtues, ways of behaviour, and modes of feeling that are ours by long inheritance. Like all good things this can become perverted and take vulgar and evil forms. Expressions such as 'un-British' or 'un-American' can express hateful attitudes of bigotry and intolerance; but those who use such terms are not usually persons who have opened their minds by any very wide or deep reading in their countries' literature [But what about the 'specialness' of the 'tongue of Shakespeare?' Why countries' here, unless it is referring to Britain's dependence on many independent ethni-cities for its 'Britishness'?: JFM] which might have given them a fuller sense of the virtues inherent in 'the British way of life' or 'the American experience'.

(45–6)

Dame Helen has gone too far. She is no longer invoking or speaking 'in the name of' her sacred value, she *names it*: being and speaking English. As such she re-opens the realm of the sign. Directly named, and not transmitted 'in the name of', the sacred can no longer, as Bakhtin has shown, support the economy, which is founded on excluding both the sacred values and their negated material foundation from the ideological stage. Directly named they become, that is, the subject of a

111

conversation, argument or debate. Rulers (Thatcher and Reagan have done this) can speak 'in the name of the old values'; but if they make the error of naming them, they will open a discussion that they will live to regret.

So it is that Dame Helen, in a move that Freud (and Lacan, too) would have appreciated, Dame Helen, this bachelor woman who has sacrificed herself to literature (her whole aim in literature nevertheless being, remember, 'to meet the man'), finds herself under the compulsion, once she has named her sacred value, to reveal the economic structure that has created that value. Following upon the passage I have just quoted, she speaks of the Third World, especially of V. S. Naipaul, just as she has already given us her repertoire of those others who have laboured to produce the 'birthright' of 'English literature', the values of the English way of life: not only the Indian Naipaul, but Swift and Joyce and Shaw, not to mention Eliot, Pound, James and Scott — from ethnicities whose values were not only once but are perpetually at war with 'British' values of the sort Dame Helen names. And by staging these writers she also centres on all those peoples that the British economy has excluded and repressed — the Irish, the Scottish, the Welsh, the Indian, etc. Once she has made her ideological values linguistic (coextensive with the English language) she has unwittingly begun to undo its borders. (Rousseau, in the *Second Discourse*, thought it improbable that language could have been invented anywhere but on an island.)

Conclusion: One way of living within ideological metaphor is to slip.

The extreme alternative model for living with ideologised metaphor is Derrida's: you attack the notion of *economy*. For Derrida there is no such thing as LANGUAGE, there are only languages which must interfere with one another. He erases the border — drawn since Kant and unwittingly repeated in Marx–Engels' model — between economic and representational values; and he writes of Bataille's dream of absolute expenditure, ruin, undermining the (gift) exchange that forms the economy of signs. Every limit drawn, every boundary, is a negation that will create an economy and a mimetic metaphysics; we cannot erase their indelible even if invisible trace, but we can re-mark them elsewhere, using marks against signs, material signifiers against verbal ones. (Rousseau's *Second Discourse* again offers both the *verbal*, logocentric negation and the material, 'deconstructive' form of negation — the line drawn around private property that founds civil society — as forms of the founding exclusions of economy. He seems to find the latter more pernicious and more deeply in error than the first, but also, perhaps the better one to overturn.)

One way we live in ideological staging of metaphor is to redo the stage.

Rousseau, Paul de Man suggests in his essay on 'Metaphor' in *Allegories of Reading* (see ch. 4, n. 3, above), intended a perpetual re-evaluation from within economies. One can attack the literal with the figurative, the figurative with the literal, one can compare the 'within' with the absoluteness of the 'without': de Man can contrast voice not with writing, but with *muteness*, humanity not with inhumanity, but with *animality*; Rousseau can write to Franquières that 'the term of the positive is not negative, it is nothing' and chide Voltaire for despairing over the Lisbon earthquake disaster by rewriting Hamlet and asking whether it is better to be or not to be at all. These are perhaps 'idealistic' or logocentric, rather than 'materialistic' solutions; and they suggest an unending series of perpetually new anamorphoses. But if we draw our initial border between 'humanity' and all the rest by means of language, then this is one possible way of living with ideology as metaphor.

The Ideological Defence of Metaphor in Literature and Psychoanalysis

In the treatment of metaphor by psychoanalysis and by those who defend the *status quo*, we are finally bound to see an ideological bias, which is that metaphor *ought* to dominate metonymy. This is the bias of all practising analysts whose aim is to adapt the ego to social conditions as they exist. One can demonstrate this in Lemaire, in Kristeva, and (see above, ch. 1) in literary criticism.

The promise of culture: future enjoyment — once presumed a sacred trust, a covenant — becomes ideological, for Lacan, with the most important of these disconnections ever culturally accomplished. This is the final divorce, at the end of the eighteenth century, between 'Goodness' and 'Happiness', that is, between the obedience to the imperatives of the superego and the promise of compensation for one's sacrifice of libidinal energy to cultural duty. The turning-point for Lacan is Kant and his quashing of eudaemonism, and the destruction of a phenomenal mode of apprehending the demands of the symbolic and moral order. Why does the subject persist in obeying the demands of the symbolic order, even beyond the promise of heterosexual love? Why, for Lacan, is the rebellion of the subject — his agressivity, which Lacan calls the futile 'Spartacist revolt' of the slave — fruitless?

Obedience to the law of return is the basis of the moral version of the symbolic order. The word as given, as voiced, comes back to us as a voice from elsewhere. Where? God, Society, the Concept? Lacan calls the force by which the subject must obey the law of return and the imperatives of a disappointing 'civilisation' that fails to calm his aggressivity the 'drive'. Metaphor powers as well as empowers.

The everlasting irony in Lacan is that there is no such thing as a pure, transcendent, ideal order. Kant tried to separate form from 'good' form by abstracting the moral order (good/bad) from it and reinventing it as a principle of freedom. But such an order is only a dream and a dream because even principles depend on the signifier if they are ever to be 'in force'. Dependence on the signifier as the form of form is therefore, unwittingly, a dependence on metaphor and its negative ideology. Metaphor unfailingly relegates the metonymic mode to the mode of myth, and to a savage myth at that, displacing it into a murderous mythic scene, where 'touching the other' is always negatively evaluated, seen in its worst light. Incest, incorporation, savage murder. The myth of the 'savage' condition into which we would fall were it not for the restraints of a metaphorically organised civilisation adds fuel to the *drive*.

The irony thus is that there *is* no Symbolic Order: only our narcissistic dream that there be one somewhere . . . beyond. A truly inaccessible Unconscious, which always must take on the guise of the Other. If a symbolic order above and beyond 'mere' signifiers could never — without those signifiers, 'fallen' miraculously from it by means of the gaze and the voice — 'communicate' its orders to us, it would be wise to reconsider the entire structure of our assumptions about the nature of the Law

114

of the Law. We have to rethink the concept that gives the image not just its form, but its 'ideal', its ideological, its 'good' form. The concept has driven us to a place where the acceleration of negation threatens to allow our collective, global annihilation and — we feel certain — 'transcendence'.

Notes

1. Walter Benjamin, 'Paris, Capital of the Nineteenth Century', in *Reflections*, tr. E. Jephcott. N.Y., Harcourt, Brace, Jovanovich, 1978, p. 148.
2. Stendhal, *Love* [1828], 1957, p. 136.
3. Mikhail Bakhtin [V. N. Vološinov], 'Discourse in Life, Discourse in Art', in *Freudianism: a Marxist Critique*, N.Y., Academic Press, 1976, p. 101.
4. See Roland Barthes, 'Myth Today', in *Mythologies*, tr. Annette Laver, N.Y., Hill and Wang, 1972, p. 113.
5. See Wilden, *System and Structure*, 168–70, for an exemplary discussion. He expands further on it in his article, 'Montage Analytic and Dialectic', *American Journal of Semiotics*, III:1, 1984, 25–47. See also MacCannell and MacCannell, *The Time of the Sign*, p. 119.
6. Since it is based on nothing but ambiguity. This is what is overlooked when one assumes that the 'phallus' has the highest value, what should be kept in view when demands for a special, revalued 'signifier' of femininity is called for. Some French feminists have attempted to remark the feminine: Irigaray gives women a 'sex' which is not one, the divided vaginal space; Derrida 'vaginalises' what had been exclusively phallic symbolisations. Certainly current social movements are attempting to ameliorate this situation, through claims for bisexuality, unisexuality, etc. as a true interchangeability of places, 'equality' exercised through the taking up, each in turn, of the capacity to experience enjoyment as the other. But interchangeability would still, structurally, be metaphoric, and it would depend on the assigning of a signifier to the feminine. In other words, the feminine would gain the prestige of having the phallus — but the underlying economy would not have been revised, and the claims of metaphor to ownership of the means of the production of meaning would go unchallenged.

If women are complicitous in this economy, acting out the metaphoric effacement of themselves through man and his 'god', they avoid the 'anxiety' of the sexual relation, which is the anxiety, in relation to an ambiguous Other, of a lack of final definition. If they have no trait or mark guaranteeing femininity, nothing granted by the Other — neither does anyone — really. If she acquiesces to the *status quo* — being unmarked — she becomes a perpetual sacrifice to the Other, whose commands are mute: destining her to absolute castration (devotion to the Other, the Saint); if she demands being marked along phallic lines, she plays the phallic mother with her the phallic child, etc. But in doing so she acquiesces to the structure of values within the cultural economy.

In an interesting article, 'Que veut une femme?' (*Ornicar?* 15, 1977, 31–40) Charles Melman describes the corollaries to our gender belief system, a system which he, following Lacan and despite his institutional arguments with him, finds structurally inadequate, incorrect. Reviewing the conflicting interpretations, among psychoanalysis, as to the young girl's means of 'access' to femininity (does one accord privilege to the aim of sexual enjoyment in the infant, to the organ (clitoris/vagina), to the timing of phallicism (primary/secondary), the locus of the address for the demand for love (mother/father), to behaviour (active/passive), etc. (p. 31), Melman wonders, with Freud, if 'woman' were not indeed specified by sustaining, maintaining a permanent wish, one that lacks a definition of who is asking and what is one asking for.

Melman answers, No: if a woman *is* asking for something, a *signifier* of her class, a symbol that could identify her through *penisneid* this is only circumstantial expression of a much more profound lack; a lack not in nature, but in culture. Culture is structured as a separation of the sexes, dividing them along permanently assymetrical lines shaped by value: ([+] masculine versus [–] feminine), but which actively prevents symmetry. Over and above these values, 'One' is set beyond them; the One is the origin of an economy of ones. Let the 'ones' within the circular economy attempt to differentiate themselves from each other or not, the final term, the value of values of all these ones is the Other, which is ultimately and always conceived as an original nay-saying (castrating) Father, the 'otherfier' of the sexual object. To reconceive the 'economic' relationship means reconstructing the role of the Other not as One, but as two, and that is not to be undertaken lightly or easily.

7. It is for this reason that Lacan is so interested in Descartes, who was able to take doubt for certainty: because he knew that the Other — God — knew, though he did not (*4FC*, 29–41).

8. The citation runs:

I would hold that no meaning given to history, based on Hegeliano–Marxist premises, is capable of accounting for this resurgence — which only goes to show that the offering to obscure gods of an object of sacrifice is something to which few subjects can resist succumbing, as if under some monstrous spell.

Lacan goes on to equate desire 'in its pure state' with the moral law,

that very desire that culminates in the sacrifice, strictly speaking, of everything that is the object of love in one's human tenderness — I would say, not only in the rejection of the pathological object, but also in its sacrifice and murder. That is why I wrote *Kant avec Sade*.
(*4FC*, 275–6)

9. Cassirer, *Rousseau, Kant and Goethe*, N.Y., Harper, 1963 (1st edn 1945), 11.

10. Published in Cambridge, Mass. by Harvard University Press as *In Defence of the Imagination*, 1980.

Part Two
Splitting the Atom: The New Order

In so far as the primary signifier is pure non-sense, it becomes the bearer of the infinitisation of the value of the subject, not open to all meanings, but abolishing them all, which is different.

(Lacan, *Four Fundamental Concepts*, 252)

6

The Symbolic Order

Freud named the three basic requirements of any civilisation —
and its discontents — as being its terms for *order, beauty* and
cleanliness. These are, in effect, so many behavioural commands
(moral imperatives, really) made to the individual who would be
a member of civil society. Anthropologists who have long subjected primitive cultures to the analysis of their hygienic practices have recently undertaken to inspect western civilisation's
rules for being clean and doing dirty work.[1] Sociologists are now
joining with aestheticians in the effort to specify western rules
for beauty beyond the marked-off realm of art.[2] Structuralists
have made major advances in analysing western codes (of
language, fashion, etc.) but no one has offered a more comprehensive viewpoint on the notion of *order* in its symbolic form
than Jacques Lacan.

Lacan's work on the terms for civil order has been largely
understood as a structuralism; that is, as an attention to the
various codes that situate our behavioural 'utterances', rendering them meaningful. His remarks on the linguistic, gender,
patriarchal, aesthetic, scientific *et al.* orders are wide-ranging
and insightful. They have, in their obvious astuteness, led his
readers to want to see one among these codes as having primacy
or mastery over the others. It is my feeling, quite to the contrary,
that Lacan's capacity to range so widely stems from something
else that is going on in his writing and which I would like to
specify here. Following Freud's triadic paradigm as he puts
culture on the couch, Lacan is interested less in the way each of
the various partial codes operates than he is in the civilising

principle that demands order in general. Operating at that level, Lacan sees three different aspects to the order-principle that this chapter lays out:

1. The way civilisation demands the *selection* and sorting of its elements into categories (via, as we have already seen, metaphoric forms of negation, selection and hierarchy) which it must officially define as stable and permanent (synchronic) although these categories are constantly beset by destabilising forces (for example, diachrony, or temporal existence, which has variable force in different kinds of societies;[3] for another, passions for transgressing borderlines — love and literature being prime examples in western life). The demand here is totalising, that is, nothing must be left out *within the civilisation's boundaries*; it must have its place.

2. The way order is *ideologised* in its everyday form. This is the way in which the contradictions between categories within the total set come to be lived out without open challenge, while experienced unconsciously as conflicts. Here civilisation requires rules for keeping contradictory categories (like the sexes) separated or else for systematically 'accommodating' them (as in the ideology of gender-blending. An acute example appears in Lévi-Strauss's early work on food. The totalising categorisation of all foodstuffs into cooked and raw, and the supplementary analogical categories of natural–processed, necessitates the creation of a third category — the rotten — or a natural processed food.) Changes or transformations in foundational categories always threaten to expose the arbitrariness of a particular order unless they are so accommodated by ideological creations of new pseudo-categories (basically imaginary identifications) that do not, in fact, disturb the underlying ones. The main point is to uphold the idea of *order*. Here we get one (false) disclosure after another in the form of a simultaneous cover-up.[4]

As the splitting and sorting accelerates in modern western society, so does the need for the concomitant ignorance (for a necessary *unconsciousness*) of potential and actual contradictions among them and for the creation of ideological cover-ups. This is what Lacan sees as *the drive* and it is the *drive* that he wishes to deconstruct. For example, in the transference, Lacan sees the identification of the patient with the analyst as just such an imaginary starting-point for the ideological cover-up of what remains, as long as the analyst is master (not only of the situation, but of himself), a 'fundamental' distinction between self and other.

3. Finally, the way in which the 'abstract' order is concretised. For Lacan, what is crucial is that the Symbolic Order is (ideally) an abstract conceptual system, a set of neutral laws, as it were, but one that, in fact, never exists *as such*. Following (rereading) Kant's 'symbolic forms' not as a set of abstract categories, but as categories, separations, splittings, that only exist *as they are experienced*, Lacan must in fact deal with concrete systems (of patriarchy, gender, language, etc.) if he wishes to speak about the Symbolic Order, but without ignoring the (ideological) drive to maintain (in the sense both of keeping and of asserting) the neutrality ('the Law') of the ordering system. The way in which he draws our attention to the ideologisation of the symbolic order, the drive to conceptualise it out of experience, is twofold:

He *reads* texts (Sade, Kant with Sade) in which certain blind-nesses to the ideological dimension of the Law are laid out. These blindnesses for Sade come from misrecognising the subject as he acts at being Kant's 'secretary' (FE 775). We must take the way in which 'laws' (especially *moral* laws) are actually experienced. Kant is, for Lacan, among the first to reveal the critical nature of 'form' in the determination of our ability to experience the concept; he reduces the object of the Law to a mere point, a 'point of emission' (FE 772). The particular form in which he experiences the 'moral' law, the repression of desire, is the voice of the Other.

He provides concrete examples of the way in which, in effect, the Law is 'enforced' in civil society, through its *police*. For Lacan, the policing of words (including the forms of politeness), the effort to contain, restrain, fix meanings and men *are* as much a part of the Law as any abstract 'spirit'.

Lacan's Symbolic Order

The *Ecrits*, as I have tried to show, have a certain discursive situation: Lacan directs his words to the analytic profession in order to persuade it of its misdirection in attempting to reconcile the ego and culture without first restructuring the narcissistic —

the love — relation between the two. We must now ask: what is the chief goal of the *Seminars*, in which Lacan lectures to students who are would-be analysts? Lacan demonstrates to the future analysts his strategies for overcoming the mystifications of institutions, including the institution of the professorat. These mystifications are the ideological *form* by means of which we apprehend the Symbolic Order. If, in the *Seminars*, Lacan does not resist culture as openly as he does in the *Ecrits*, his reasons for this are part of a strategy aimed at reminding the student, forcefully, of the awesome power of the Symbolic. Lacan introduces and reintroduces the Symbolic Order in the *Seminars* to demonstrate its *effects* on the psyche. Lacan claims that his goal is to try to create a 'new geometry' (*Scilicet* 6/7, 40)[5] in which Symbolic/Imaginary/Real would be in a relation of equality, figured by the Borromean knot, in which each 'circle' is intercepted by and looped through each of the others, on whose integrity it is dependent. Nonetheless, as a teacher of those who would try to *cure*, he must underscore the very real domination — in modern culture — of the Symbolic over the two other registers (Imaginary and Real).

Like the American founder of 'semiotic', Charles Sanders Peirce, Lacan noted the tendency of the symbol to become the prototype of the other sign-relations (icon and index for Peirce; metaphor and metonymy for Lacan). Like Peirce, Lacan never openly expressed whether this tendency for the symbol to dominate should be evaluated negatively or positively: it is undeniably a *fact* of the human, civilised order. The symbolic has unquestionable claims for being that which defines 'humanity' since symbols are a human-specific co-creation. Symbols set us apart from all other sentient beings since they require a common interhuman recognition for their existence, and a mutual, 'conventional' agreement about their significance. Speech is the primary example, as are other forms of social intercourse. But in their tendency to dominate all other modes (e.g. imaginary and real) symbols also have an inherent tendency to move beyond the realm of recognition and conscious agreement. *Unconscious*, they become powerful systems that transcend, pre-date and pre-order those humans who now can be seen less as the makers and masters of the symbol than its servants, less users of symbols as tools than themselves mere instruments for perpetuating the existence of symbols: 'speech' cedes priority to 'language' as a general system; a particular relation to another becomes a set of kinship rules, empowered to situate and systematise, in advance, all possible forms of relations. Mutual desire, mediated by an agreed-upon symbol becomes a general will — a will to genre, to classify, order, organise — that not only renders mutual desire unconscious, but effectively precludes it.

As the Symbolic Order, civilisation (in its modern version at least) is a vast unconscious. But no 'unconscious' can force the consciousness to work for it, it can extract no energy or labour from it without having an executive arm, without, that is, appearing in (twisted) form to that consciousness. The question becomes not so much *how* humans become dominated by the forms they themselves create as *why*? What does the symbolic promise in exchange for the giving-up of conscious desire?

We know that, for Lacan, the traditional versions of what the symbolic order offers — its *ideological* forms, as 'morality', 'religion', 'culture', 'civilisation', 'Oedipus', have played out, exhausted their traditional powers of incentive. We live, we are told, in a post-religious, amoral world, and Oedipus is waning. Even our sense of living in a world of 'laws' seems threatened less by the themes of pity than of terror. If the Symbol is to continue to dominate the other modes, it clearly must now create new ideological forms for maintaining and perpetuating its dominance.

Lacan has found the radical mode for this new ideological form of the (involuntary) gift to lie in the realm of *value*. What the Symbolic promises to the human in exchange for his gift of conscious desire to it is its positive evaluation of him. Lacan writes that, in reality, the Symbolic is no-thing; the 'primary signifier is pure non-sense' (*4FC*, 252); but it is that nothing which doubly splits the human from not simply his so-called 'own' desires, but, more importantly, from the other humans without whom desire literally makes no sense. Giving him a place in the Order promises to 'evaluate' him. And so it does; it gives him infinite value, rather cheaply bought, since he, like it, is no-thing. The trick is that nothing divided by nothing yields not nothing, but infinity: '[the pure non-sense of the signifier] becomes the bearer of the infinitisation of the value of the subject, not open to all meanings, but abolishing them all, which is different' (*4FC*, 252).

As a critic, it is Lacan's goal to make these new forms of domination 'strange', to make us feel again the power of our productions — including the power they have *over* us. It is a power enforced by the most familiar things. The way in which a Symbolic system dominates our desires is by means of the intersubjective mode of substituting *values* for *meanings*.

Until now, the psyche has always tended to relate to the 'Symbolic Order' as either a benign or malignant force — as a subject (a deity) with a 'will'. This has clearly changed — or has it? That is the question Lacan's work puts to us, as he demonstrates the *âme* (soul in the most subjective spiritual sense) even in the heart of our modern amorality (*âmorality*). We have never really overcome the intersubjective; the narcissistic relation of self to code has not yet been altered. To do so would indeed be revolutionary. A code once seen as arbitrary is a code open to being changed, like a language experienced as strange by being reflected in a foreign translation, one that can no longer regard *its* grammar as universal. It is the genuine absence of universality in codes that the order-principle is most driven to cover up, and the intersubjective mode of responding to it as to a call is the most effective mode of doing the covering.

The Critical Reception of Lacan's 'Symbolic Order': The Other

Critics of various persuasions have offered ambivalent responses to the 'Symbolic Order' in Lacan's work — to that order which we, as human users of symbols, have, *between us*, made, and which we see now also makes us. Not only ambivalence, but outright confusion on the part of Lacan's readers is the hallmark of how they evaluate the Symbolic, and critical attitudes also tend to be aligned with the gender class of the critic. Men can and often do see the pernicious effects of an overly patriarchal imagery surrounding the Symbolic, but they fail to question its claims to priority and domination in general; women are quite openly hostile to an Order that by definition precludes positive, marked recognition of their gender class. But rare is the critic of either sex who questions as radically as Lacan himself did the idea of Order, of *one* universal order, the *drive* toward order.

In what follows I attempt to situate the spectrum of critical attitudes toward the symbolic both by comparing them to each other, and by placing them alongside Lacan's reading of Kant. A double perspective emerges:

1. Lacan is intent on breaking the intersubjective mode of relating to culture, of seeing it as the 'Other', or at least a uni-personal, single-sexed, 'Other'. Whenever Lacan's readers fail to see this intention in Lacan they tend to overvalue the 'Other' and to acquiesce in its alienating power. There is also a failure to apprehend the source from which the symbolic derives its power as the splitting of the self from the other, the diversion of libidinal energies to serve the end of perpetuating the order. Hence the correctness of the feminist attack on the masculist symbols which give us a sense of the Other and on the tendency of real men to identify with the Other, but the incorrectness of their support for those things that reinforce divisions between the sexes, a splitting upon which the powerful drive of the Symbolic depends.

2. Lacan shows us, via his reading of Kant, the power the Symbolic Order has to blind and bind us to it — even the most perceptive among us. Kant drew our attention to the trans-cendence of symbolic forms; he thus opened the way for us to treat these forms as flexible codes, subject to change. For Lacan, this is a major step beyond the categorical mind of the Greeks, the idea of 'unmoved Being'. Kant opens, technically, the 'call to conscience', the intersubjective mode of relation to the Symbolic: in the end, Kant must experience the Law not as pure code, but as an 'inner voice'. So although Kant opens the way to de-personalising form, to freeing us from apprehending it as a distorted version first of our bodies and then of our egos, he does not, finally, reduce the moral code to 'mere form', without phenomenal and intersubjective content. This is perhaps, nearly impossible.

The Critics

It is instructive to look at the way readers have *taken*, have received, and have responded to the Symbolic Order as explicated by Lacan in the *Ecrits*. I have excluded from my consideration here the reader who has attempted the most radical semiotic redefinition, the most critical re-framing of the frame of the Symbolic Order, Jacques Derrida.[6]

The first wave of Lacan criticism accepted a partial identification between the Symbolic Order and Civilisation, or Oedipal culture. Readers considered Lacan's ability to synthesise the advances in the human, cultural, sciences with Freud's insights as his major contribution to psychoanalysis. Thus, the Symbolic Order is generally seen by his early readers basically in the form of the patriarchal ideological order, built upon the castration complex, the necessary and normalising mechanism of civilisation: When Culture is seen as a kindly father, the Symbolic Order likewise appears benign. Remember that the function of the symbolic Father is, according to Lacan, 'fundamentally to unite (and not set in opposition) a desire and the law' (*EE*, 321). Civilisation is the work of the law, which is, in Lacan's reconfirmation of Freud's insight in *Kant avec Sade*, always the repression of a desire.

In this most benign, 'civilising' interpretation, the Symbolic Order stands in the role of the mediator: as the law, it restricts desire; as the mediator who must also assure procreation, it also — selectively — accommodates desire to the law which denies it. The Other, Lacan writes, performs the function of providing a 'viable, temperate relationship of one sex to the other . . . outside love' (*XX*, I, 12). In the example of the promise, the given word, untamed, disorderly desire for the other sex can be shaped and ordered by a vow of fidelity, organised, at another level of structure, as the marriage vow, to 'love, honour and obey'. The analyst would then be, as Piron puts it, the representative of the symbolic order, taking the place of the Other, as a 'third party witness to the truth, the guarantor of good faith whom we always invoke when we address ourselves to someone in an effort at coinciding with what is absolutely true' (Lemaire, 217; also above, Ch. 1).

Charged thus with the aura of the positive side of Oedipus, this reading of the Symbolic Order in Lacan tends to emphasise its work as a *medium*, and mediator, thereby minimising the disruptive and disconnecting side we have been at pains, in our reading of the *Ecrits*, to evoke. But it fails to explain adequately why then Lacan links it not to the Superego, but to the

128

'Unconscious'. In Freud, the unconscious is the scene of (illegitimate) sexual connections; made in the unconscious, these are
necessarily repressed by unconsciousness, under the censorship
of the superego. But in Lacan, the Symbolic Order, where negation occurs, would present a very different face for the unconscious, more equivalent to *Kultur* (or civilisation) in Freud than
to the idea of a location where freewheeling primary processes
operate.

Moreover, the unconscious in Freud appears to operate as
having an explicitly illegitimate sexual content. The Symbolic
Order is the realm of Law. Readers of Lacan stress, as he (ironically) did, the unconscious as this scene of cutting and censorship, not the scene of connection. Its imperatives are negative.
For Lacan, in the Symbolic Order is the site of distinction, negation and disconnection which are an unconscious because they
cancel or put combinations under erasure.

In an Oedipal, civilised guise, the division or split required by
culture is made in terms of a (false) promise of a future combination. But in fact culture is the realm of the categorical,
where distinctions, generic ones in particular, are made,
rendering the promise of combination a false one, as Lacan
repeatedly noted, in his assertion of the lack of sexual relations.

Freud's unconscious 'knows no negation', allowing all of its
elemental components to cohabit side by side, as it were, without
distinction. The Symbolic Order in Lacan is therefore the
unconscious at a different level: it is a *moral* order. (Readers of
Durkheim are already familiar with this notion of the moral,
rather than the immoral, unconscious.)

Literature, the Symbolic Order and Criticism

I have already pointed to the psychoanalytic support for the
'moral' Symbolic Order. What I now look at is the ambivalence
of literary critics in respect to it. Critics have tended to emphasise Lacan's Symbolic Order at the expense of not only the
Freudian scene, but the two other orders (imaginary and real).

Under pressure from Lacan's concepts, literary criticism, the
reading of literature, *becomes* a culture criticism. This is so at
least in part because literature is one of the finest available

models for developing ways of comprehending the Unconscious (Symbolic) Order in its (necessarily) imaginary, sensible form. The 'Freudian', the sexual 'unconscious' is never reached *as such* by Freud, or by anyone else: Lacan pointed this out very carefully. Our only intimations of it appear in the narrative, linguistic and already highly censored form of the dream-work, in the figurative modes of condensation and displacement. As readers of this narrative form we are on the other side of the curtain; as literary analysts, we have been trained to attend to the level of the signifier and not the sign (intended for someone); we have read not literary 'content' or 'substance', but 'significant' form.

And yet, and yet . . . have we understood form properly? This is the question Paul de Man (and Bakhtin)[7] asked us; but no one asked it more elaborately and eloquently than Lacan. Form, figure, curtains the body; cuts us off from it. But, Lacan asks again and again, why do we love this deletion? Do we have to give our love to a mere form? And he answers just as repeatedly, we do when it is 'good' form: beauty, wisdom, etc., in short, *moral* form. Literary form, closely followed by literary theory and criticism, has been in the process of detaching itself from 'good, moral' form at least since the close of the eighteenth century. As such, not only the methods of reading through texts and narratives, but the very history of literary criticism ought to have made us the most able and flexible of general cultural analysts, the most critical of the Symbolic tendency to present itself in beautiful, orderly, moral forms.

One has to wonder, then, at the enthusiasm of some literary critics for the Oedipal, moral version of the Symbolic Order,[8] since it is perhaps only in literature, in fiction that the positive unconscious scene, the scene of connection, has 'appeared': plays have more than one scene . . . And if they are sometimes hierarchically arranged, by a would-be Symbolic Order (e.g. the unities), that order can always be violated — on stage.

Freud found the conscious *ego* to be the arena of the formalisations — and repressions — that shape our world. But for Lacan, although the ego is their starting-point, formalisations, especially in the mode of *choices*, emanate from the Symbolic Order (in Lacan's interpretation of Freud's *Verwerfung*),[9] which comes 'before' (in the hierarchical sense) the ego. For Lacan, the symbolic is the realm of pure form, devoid of phenomenal content, and it organises for us both the imaginary and the real.

The symbolic is supposed to be a form *without phenomenal content*, such that it is divested of all the inessential features — feelings, images, objects — that might obscure its overall intent, the symbolic reorganisation and reconstruction of desire. If Culture began by alienation, the alienation of desire, separating, dividing and distinguishing, barring the relationship of self to other that follows from sheer contiguity, it should go on about the business of recombining them *according to the law*, and independently of passions, emotions, etc. It is supposed to operate, that is, according to *principles*. As Anthony Wilden puts it, in *System and Structure*:

> The Other is not a person, but a principle; the locus of the 'law of desire', the locus of the incest-prohibition and the phallus. According to Lacan, the Other — mythically represented in Freud by the Symbolic father of *Totem and Taboo* — is the only place from which it is possible to say 'I am who I am'. The paradox of identity and autonomy which this involves — identical to or identified with what? — puts us in the position of desiring what the Other desires: we desire what the Other desires we desire.
>
> (22–3)

The reader of Lacan is, however, not as free as he or she might like to be to see this aspect of the Symbolic Order, or *Kultur* in Freud's terminology, as a pure gain: the ethical triumph of law and civilisation. The law gains energy for civilisation at the expense of the relation of self and other; it is this relation that must be sacrificed. Anything can look like a benefit from the point of view of the totality, an economy of pluses and minuses, gains and losses. The surplus value gained by culture is experienced solely as loss for the self, which really depends on others.

It is not easy to see the pernicious aspects of the symbolic. Anthony Wilden is one of Lacan's most astute commentators, and a politically sensitive writer. For example, he is conspicuously conscientious about not making judgemental comparisons between 'civilised' and 'uncivilised' peoples (Wilden's terms), in his efforts to explicate societies organised around metaphoric ('hot' — modern) and metonymic ('cold' — traditional) modes. Yet one finds a subtle valorisation of the Symbolic Order in Wilden's text, effected by his contrasting it with the imaginary. For Wilden the imaginary is plenitude, filled with positive images which necessarily distort and mask the reality of human relationships because it is also the realm of hidden form (as in Freud), the master cultural form, opposition. It is the task, in Lacan as Wilden reads him, of the symbolic to master the imaginary, which is the domain of all ideology, illusion and mythification. Shortcircuiting the modelling and mediating function of the Symbolic — which is what the Imaginary, Wilden tells us, does — allows us to fall prey to those delusions with which we are all too familiar in modern life: images of the relationship between the sexes distort the reality of these relations, etc. (The errors of the Imaginary, as distinct from the Symbolic, as we have already seen, are most egregious in relation to the self, where in the form of the Ideal (imagined) Ego, the self falls into a binarism, an endless oscillation between seeing oneself as the exact equal of other selves, and exactly opposed to them: a circle of identity and opposition that the thirdness of the Other, the Symbolic Order breaks, thereby refounding the social order on a different basis. This is consistent with Lacan's many allusions to the 'breaking' of the anthropological circle.)

The difference between the mythic Imaginary and the Symbolic Order is that the symbolic mediates the actual relationship of self and other, by forcing the desire between self and other to go through the circuit of the symbolic, where it is *rearranged* and *reordered* on a new basis. Wilden writes:

Behind the Symbolic lies the notion of mediated (unconscious) desire. The word translated 'instinct' in Freud clearly never meant instinct for him, and may very well be translated 'desire'. Moreover, Freud points out that there are no 'instinctual impulses' (*Triebregungen*) 'in' the unconscious, only 'representatives of desire' (*Triebpräsentanz*). (Consider the situation of the ethnic minorities in England, France, or the United States, for whom all desires are coded white.) We therefore desire to TAKE THE PLACE of the Other in desire.

132

When all is said and done then, we do not desire objects, we desire desire itself.

(22-3)

But Wilden's critique of the Imaginary is only one face of an ultimately uncritical view of the Symbolic Order. When Wilden finds any specific application of the Symbolic Ordering of desire to race, to psychosis and to the family as 'culture-bound, since it depends on a patriarchal ideology' he insists they are 'in fact, Imaginary in Lacan's own terms' (Wilden, 26). This is in fact the case, but as we have seen above, the Symbolic Order, unless it manifests itself as the Other, takes form, is seen or heard, received as an image, cannot be effective, has no instruments for its operation. Wilden finds the predominance of the Imaginary a devastating condition for human affairs, and it is. Where there is no Other, he writes, there are only 'others' — imaginary others who fulfil only one role or another, to be identical with or to be opposed to oneself. For Wilden only something he associates with the 'natural' state of affairs, the otherness of pure difference that can only exist outside language, is the alternative to a human, that is fully symbolic, order.

It is impossible not to notice that it is the Symbolic Order that feminists (although Wilden is an avowed feminist), have tended to attack. They often valorise the imaginary. Certainly, that is a major direction of feminism, very succinctly put in Laura Mulvey's (1975) critique of our cinematic pleasures:

The paradox of phallocentrism in all its manifestations is that it depends on the image of the castrated woman to give order and meaning to its world. An idea of woman stands as lynch pin to the system: it is the lack that produces the phallus as a symbolic presence, it is her desire to make good the lack that the phallus signifies. Recent writing . . . has not sufficiently brought out the importance of the representation of the female form in a symbolic order in which, in the last resort, it speaks castration and nothing else. To summarise briefly: the function of woman in forming the patriarchal unconscious is two-fold, she first symbolises the castration threat by her real absence of a penis and second thereby raises her child into the

133

symbolic. Once this has been achieved, her meaning in the process is at an end, it does not last into the world of law and language except as a memory which oscillates between memory of maternal plenitude and memory of lack. Both are posited on nature (or on anatomy in Freud's famous phrase). Woman's desire is subjected to her image as bearer of the bleeding wound, she can exist only in relation to castration and cannot transcend it. She turns her child into the signifier of her own desire to possess a penis (the condition, she imagines, of entry into the symbolic). Either she must gracefully give way to the word, the Name of the Father and the Law, or else struggle to keep her child down with her in the half-light of the imaginary. Woman then stands in patriarchal culture as signifier for the male other, bound by a symbolic order in which man can live out his phantasies and obsessions through linguistic command by imposing them on the silent image of woman still tied to her place as bearer of meaning, not maker of meaning.[10]

The Symbolic Order, if based on the name of the Father and the sacrificial word, is, it seems, equally based on the exclusion of the woman.

Women feel as trapped in the Symbolic Order as they did in the patriarchal household. Guerrilla tactics of disruption, images of 'breaking out', mark a great deal of the feminist literature on Lacan and psychoanalysis: the most eminent example is Julia Kristeva's espousal of the 'semiotic', the 'rhythmic', and feminine *jouissance*, as forces for breaking the symbolic hold.

Mulvey incites women to protest at not too much imagery, but too little of the right sort: where, Mulvey asks, is the image of the 'sexing of the female infant and her relationship to the symbolic, the sexually mature woman as non-mother, maternity outside the signification of the phallus, the vagina . . .' (7). Too much representation of woman for male pleasure, not enough representation of women in terms *not* organised tacitly by the negations of the Symbolic Order.[11]

So with the same conclusion as Wilden — the overvaluing of patriarchal ideology — we have exactly opposed reasons for opposing patriarchy: for Wilden, patriarchy is only an imaginary version of the Symbolic Order, for Mulvey, it *is* the Symbolic Order.

If you see the Symbolic Order as merely coercive, as Mulvey does, not as benign mediator or broker, the linkage Lacan makes between the structure and aim of civilisation and the process of symbolisation is obscured, just as it is exaggeratedly rationalised in a schema that sees its positive 'civilising' qualities alone. The only possible response would have to be disruption, or else resignation.

What means for disruption have been advocated? Kristeva speaks of lifting repression a little, to image forth the woman at the threshold between the imaginary and the symbolic, but never actually crossing it: for her, we are *in* the Symbolic Order, for her the equivalent of grammar, and if we are to remain human, we must stay within it, which does not preclude nostalgia to another more animal life, a different earthier condition.[12] Mulvey claims that destroying the various forms of male pleasure gained by seeing women through the male-framed gaze would constitute the means of subverting the symbolic subversion of the imaginary, identified here with the woman.

But even in the feminist critique, the advocacy is that of doing away with constraints, arbitrary constraints on one gender and it never really addresses the structure of the Symbolic Order itself — its thirdness, its supplement to the self/other dialogue, the self/other glance, its forming, directing and shaping their exchange.

Take the gaze in Lacan. Once he names this term, which he openly admits taking from Sartre, critics, especially feminists, are quick to respond. Women have been subjected to the male gaze; for ever, it seems, they have been framed by, trapped by, it. Now a glimmer of hope, of liberation appears: Mulvey's solution is to disrupt the male gaze by interrupting the pleasure of the visual, entitling one of her sections 'Destruction of Pleasure as a Radical Weapon' (7).

Could it be that simple? In Lacan there is no escape from the process of symbolisation, which is essentially the process of alienation, in the relationship of self to other, and self to self. In the glance, he writes, we see the other. But because we can see him or her, we also know the other can see us: we can take the point of view of the other, in a transitive relationship. This is the moment, in Hegelian terms, of 'recognition'. And it is this moment that falls to the power of the Other, who enters the scene immediately to disrupt this transitivity: a *third* point of view, that which is constitutive of the Lacanian *regard*, arises. We see ourselves being seen and seeing. It is this third dimension which creates the specifically human (alienated) condition (*I*, xviii, 245–50).[13]

But the only *power* this fictional 'transcendental' third party has arises from those subjected to its gaze, from their *way* of relating to it: as It, as He, as Other. If they overvalue it, deferring to it as higher, more all-seeing, wiser, more knowledgeable, they are subject to it. If they resist giving it ultimate value, a different way of forming the tie between them could result. But no matter what attitude they take towards it, they can no longer assume they refer only to each other: they *must* also refer themselves to it. For Lacan, only the *form* of reference to the Other can be modified, not the fact of its existence, for it is coextensive with the human condition: the 'Spartacist revolt' is useless.

Lacan's work outlines strategies of resistence along five major lines:

1. Resisting its personification through a diminution of the 'field of the ego': the aim of progress in analysis, he writes, is not the aggrandising of the field of the ego. It is not the reconquest by the ego of its unknown *frange*; it is a real reversal (*renversement*), a displacement, like a minuet executed between ego and id (*I*, xviii, 257).

2. Resisting its (economic) institutions, which are *in fact* the only way in which the Symbolic Order 'communicates' its will to us. Lacan is most interesting where he sees how the purely negative laws of the Unconscious Symbolic Order are given their concrete manifestation. For Freud, only narration could give us, he thought, indirect access to the land behind the dream. For Lacan the unconscious can be read elsewhere, otherwise than in the way the symbolic writes it: it can be read through the landscape, especially the urban landscape that is before our eyes — Baltimore in the early morning, as the famous quote goes, is his 'definition' of the unconscious. (Another famous example, is of course, Lacan's 'urinary laws of the segregation of the sexes'. The arbitrary sorting of children into what we assume are the

abstract categories of gender via Symbolic Orderings (linguistic persons, active and passive principles, etc.) are *effected* by means of very concrete institutions: separate toilets, as I tried to show in Chapter 1, in Lacan's parable of the children arriving at their station by train only to learn that they had arrived at 'Ladies' (his version) and 'Gentlemen' (her version) or at the beginning of the 'war between the sexes'.)

Lacan's putting the matter in this way necessarily raises our suspicions. Are the institutions the effect, really, of the laws, or the other way around? His answer is that to say the material signifier, always *en route* to metaphoric elevation, is 'primary' is true, and it is also not true, since the very capacity of the signifier to metaphorise also hangs on the *principle* of division which is unquestioningly, unfailingly obeyed. Distinctions 'must' be made. The principle is that of negation: whatever has to do with the actual body, especially those parts that deal with reproduction, must be denied access to psychic life except in ideal, imagistic or symbolic form. To make this clearer, I return once more to the example of the toilets. The social practice of not exposing the mature genitalia to members of the opposite sex in public places is a taboo maintained by a concrete social — and effectively policed — institution — of separate toilets. Without actual ocular knowledge of another's genitals, one can have no real *proof* of the other's sex. Thus, according to Goffman and equally to Lacan is *gender* born: from the signifiers that hide, displace or cancel the actual 'sex'. From this absence flows the development of an ideology of gender (see Introduction above) that is 'founded' by our lack of knowledge of 'sex'; we have already seen how Lacan insists that the psyche admits only tokens (signifiers) of reproduction, and never the sexual act itself. But if something so 'abstract' as gender is not a *foundational* (that hidden *fundamentum* again) part of the Symbolic Order, but is in fact a social custom elevated to the level of a rule, then what is the composition of the Symbolic Order itself?

3. Resisting a reading of it as the realm of judgement and moral value: no matter whether we take it as the realm of ultimate Goodness, or malignancy, morality always takes the form of the sacrifice. Lacan's most explicit discussion of this area of resistance is given in his essay on Kant and Sade.

4. Lacan will show that what must be undermined is not the

Symbolic Order as an edifice, a solid, stolid stable structure of categorical pigeonholes — a set of arrangements, but as a universal movement, a *drive*. For it is clear that there is nothing in the Symbolic Order other than one principle: that of division and polarisation (negative/positive). And this principle of division is a force, a power, an energy: a splitting and a fission.[14]

5. Finally, the resistance to the transference (modelled as a relation between egos), and a re-evaluation of the *objet a*, outside the *drive*.

I first take the problem of the *morality* of the Symbolic Order, the morality, that is, of *form*.

The Morality of Forms: *'Kant avec Sade'* or Sacrifice Beyond Oedipal Promise

> Her parted lips locked themselves with the determination to be employed no longer. She would forget everything, she would repeat nothing, and when as tribute to her successful application of her system, she began to be called a little idiot, she tasted a pleasure new and keen.
>
> (Henry James, *What Maisie Knew*)

Feminine disruption of the Symbolic may consist in nothing more than deafening the ears to the voice, resisting the seduction of speech. Perhaps the necessary first move is to stop listening — to the voice from on high (or on the radio).

If we take the Symbolic Order as I have been doing, as a new moment or 'advance' in the structure of civilisation, then we can be sure that Lacan is not about to overlook its *Unbehangen* as well as its gains. We need to reread Culture, principles and the law not through neo-Kantian eyes, but through Freud's once more. I therefore find Mulvey's suggestion that the gain of *pleasure* offered by images of women as they are framed by the Symbolic Order is what must be disrupted and destroyed quite a Kantian, but a not unproblematic proposition. On the one hand, disturbing the *economy* of pleasure *is* a radically critical action; but on the other, it does nothing, in Mulvey's case, to undo the divisiveness of that order, it prolongs 'the battle of the sexes'. Is advocacy of the 'destruction of a pleasure' really subversive of the Symbolic Order, at least of the Symbolic Order not seen as a mediation and accommodation of imaginary and real modes? I think we need to proceed very carefully in the treatment of the Symbolic Order: it is brought into play *by* subverting pleasure.

By reading Lacan on the Symbolic Order through his comments on Kant I think we shall get a better sense of the continuous, compelling — and destructive — activity of the 'moral' *unconscious*, the Symbolic Order. It is a force, not a state of being; it drives us, rather than the other way round. The Lacan text I choose for this rereading, *Kant avec Sade*, is one that has evoked little commentary. (It is not included in the selection from the *Ecrits* translated by Alan Sheridan; what little has been written on it is confusing. Catharine Clément, in her *Lives and Legends of Lacan*, an informative if journalistic account, writes of this essay — the only one of the *Ecrits* actually written for publication rather than as a speech — that although Lacan begins by noting their temporal affinity, he 'shows, in rather elliptical fashion, that Sade is the absolute opposite of Kant' (209).[15] I hope to situate the text in the culture-critical mode of Lacan's work.

Kant

In contrast to all other versions of the Law that depend on *feeling* or sentiment, Kant placed the moral realm beyond subjection to 'sense', 'eudaemonism' — particularly to the 'feminine' appeal of virtue — beyond Shaftesbury and all the rest. With Kant we (almost) attain pure law. After Kant, we *know* that we do not and should not obey the Law of the Symbolic for sentimental and ideological reasons, for 'ends' for moral prizes dangled before us — the 'lady fair' we shall win (or become if we are women), the child who will carry our 'name' (or compensate for its loss, if we are women). These are no longer the bearers of the Symbolic's appeal.

Lacan forces us to wonder. Kant 'hears voices' (the inner voice of conscience). His faith in the Law requires closing the eye and opening the ear. He is still subject to its 'appeal' (*appel*, 'call'). Do the extremes of apathy and impersonalisation finally meet? Lacan places Kant *with* not against (*avec* not *contre*) Sade. There is a Kantian quality to the primacy of the Law and the absence of pleasurable feeling in Sade, just as there is a certain sadistic pleasure in Kant's keeping the thing-in-itself covered up, out of reach. In fact, Lacan finds, Kant experiences the law through recourse to an inter-subjective mode — *the* intersubjective mode: the voice, speech. Sade failed to resist the eye, Kant the call, the power of the voice. Is Kant complicitous in initiating a cover-up, an ideological *drive*? He may have opened the way for perhaps a greater degree of misery for the subject than Oedipus did . . .

The Destruction of Pleasure as perhaps a Not So Radical Weapon

In *Kant avec Sade* Lacan, as usual, proffers an historical point of view: with Kant there is a major turning-point in the way human beings conceive of the highest, the supreme, the sovereign Good. Antiquity's version of the supreme Good — towards which men tend as towards their greatest possible happiness — is best summed up (elsewhere, in *God and the Jouissance of Woman*) by Aristotle's notion of 'unmoved Being'. If our greatest Good and happiness is in the *image* of a self-contained, inanimate Being, it is because we ourselves fall far short of it, we have indeed fallen from such a state, and the only source of our animation is our movement back towards this state of Being. Indeed, Lacan finds, that the imagery of Unmoved Being is the source of the *anima* (or soul) which is the only thing that could so move us; and as such, it is also the frame for our love relations, which Lacan re-spells 'amour', since happiness — which can only be found, of course, in love — is the only plausible motivational force. We are 'moved' toward 'the Good Old God of Aristotle'.

What Kant's revolution brought, Lacan finds, is a revolution in the ideological goal of happiness. We can no longer view our lives from the standpoint of their aim or goal, organising them toward a finalised end. Stumbling over the inexpressibility, in German, of a certain phrase — in French, 'on est bien dans le bien' (the English would be something like 'one feels good in

140

goodness'; Lacan writes the German as '*Man fühlt sich wohl im Guten*' FE 766) — Kant found himself forced to disengage *happiness* from the Good.

Well before Freud, Kant discovered that the the 'law of the Good' in Antiquity is invalid, a pleasure principle that undoes its aim in the act of its institution. No subjective ethical will can be defined by such a law, no phenomenon can be authorised by a constant relationship to pleasure. For Kant, *das Gute* has to be reborn as a *moral* law, no longer apprehended in the sensuous, visual mode of pleasure it only 'signifies' (FE 767).

How, then, one asks, is the moral law apprehended by consciousness if it has no aesthetically presented form? It is, Kant finds, reduced to a mere index, it is indicated by an interior *subjective* relationship. We *hear* inside us the voice of the commandments, rather than seeing outside us a pleasurable goal. The Good must, according to Kant, divest itself of all phenomenal content, it must propose itself across and against all objects that would place conditions on it. It is only in this way that it can attain the status of the concept, that is, of *universal value* and can therefore become not a mere regulative principle, but a *moral* LAW (766–7).

As a universal concept, the LAW OF THE GOOD must be a value excluded from the merely empirical world — either of objects or of feelings. Kant is particularly concerned, Lacan finds, to exclude the dimension of pathos from the law. Any feeling a subject can suffer (passion) in relation to an object must be seen as 'pathological' and must also therefore be excluded from the universality of the concept. It is in this way that Kant liberates the moral field, by rejecting the pathological, eliminating all account taken of passion, compassion, etc. Kant thereby creates the freedom of the moral will: 'The will is not obligated except to end by its practice all reasons that are not in the maxim itself' (767). This is the latent moral imperative, Lacan finds, of the Other. In other words, the LAW refers only to itself for its guide, and its tautological aim is to be itself: 'I am that I am, liberty. Sade, too, posits the Other's liberty (771).

The effect of the concept of the Good in Kant, then, is not, as in Aristotle, that of a counterweight, a positive attraction towards rather than merely the tendency to fall away from. In

Kant it is what Lacan calls an 'anti-weight', a purely negative function aimed at denying pleasure: 'a glance at this Good renders one's pleasures less respectable'. (A fine literary example of this kind of ethical will can be seen in the end of Henry James's *The Portrait of a Lady*, where Isabel Archer, amorously approached — even embraced and kissed Casper Goodwood — decides to fulfil her promise to her stepdaughter, Pansy, to return to her. Clearly re-marking the ethical over the (presumably) pleasurable moment, Isabel is at the same time making the decision for a symbolic ordering at another level, obligating herself not to a natural child, 'civilised' product of the heterosexuality sacrifice in its first stages aims at, but to an artificial 'child', one created, for her, entirely out of symbolic arrangements. Interestingly, it is also at this point that the novel ends, leaving a blank in Isabel's life. We can have absolutely no intuition of what will happen to this Kantian woman.)

The renunciation of pleasure is the critical moment for Lacan. For at the point where the subject glances toward the concept, fulfilling the maxim (in Isabel's case the promise to return, keeping her given word), the subject is facing NO OBJECT, only words, to which objects have already always been sacrificed. That, Lacan writes, is when the subject encounters a LAW. The LAW, required to be valid for all cases in order for it to have any value at all, to have what is required of the concept, universal validity and applicability, can take no account of particular circumstance, specific phenomena, the emotions surrounding it.

This is also the critical moment for Lacan, where he begins his own critical musing. What motivates Kant, he asks, to hold the object always out of reach of any aesthetic transcendental determination? As a reader of Freud he must read Kant's extreme division of the will from the *pathos*. Given his understanding of civilisation, the realm of laws which are always repressions of desire, the renunciation of the object can be seen as a diversion of libidinal energy towards another — reformed — enjoyment. The enjoyment by the Other? Not pleasure, but joy, a joy Lacan terms 'impotent'.

For Lacan, *symbolic* thought is the concept without any empirical intuition. Symbolic thinking releases the concept from all intuition of an object. It is only an operator, 'In language it corresponds to the operation which transforms the natural given, negates it, and which generates and mediates formal values' (Lemaire, citing Ortigues, p. 55). The concept in language is equivalent to God. Similarly, the concept in Kant, the universal value, is equivalent to God, but not a God oriented towards happiness, or 'feeling good' but simply towards being a universal value, I am that I am.

What is the effect? What is, in practice, the Symbolic Order as a *principle*, versus the Symbolic Order as marriage broker, mediating Father, stand-in (and replacement for) the mutual recognition between subjects? Lacan cites Kant's own example of the difference between the gibbet as a regulative device threatening punishment for the fulfilment of one's passions, and the law, which forecloses them (782). The Law is not the police. Kant's system would eliminate the subject and all its *pathos* (this is the healthy side of Kant) from the application of the law.

Can we really tell the difference between the Law and the police if the Law transcends empirical and sensuous apprehension of its working? Yes and no, since Kant does reject the aesthetic but not the verbal 'symbolic' mode of apprehending the Law.

But Lacan wants to know what actually motivates Kant. Indeed, every law is a repression of a desire, but we have to ask, What is the nature of the desire repressed? Kant 'breaks' the circular law of pleasure, it is true, but in his tantalisation of the subject with an object always just out of reach, he is also acting sadistically and we need to know why. For Kant, the police, the state, the empirical manifestations of morality are not the LAW. The only real manifestation of the law is the *repression of desire* (782): the freedom to die, to desire in vain (783).

Is the absence of desire, then, the end of alienation, or a further deepening of it, one more step in rendering desires unconscious? Is the conceptual God of Kant really a God without its own peculiar joys? (Lacan warns us to avert our gaze from picturing God's enjoyment.) And does Kant accomplish, really, the creation of a morally effective counter-weight to the positive attraction of the classical Good, or merely induce our (unconscious) attraction for its opposite, Evil? Evoking literary history, Lacan speculates that it may be Kant who set us on a route (played out through the nineteenth century) towards finding *happiness* only in Evil (765).

Sade

In Sade, we never see desire, only the object of Law. Ironically, for Lacan, Sade is an almost textbook illustration of the *Critique of Practical Reason* in reverse. As in Kant, a certain object is held out, beyond the limits of perception; but another object *is* unveiled: Dasein as agent of torture (772). Lacan reads Sade as excluding one particular object, drawing only one boundary he will not transgress, will not violate, so even here a (Kantian) limit is reached: 'Sade . . . clôt l'affaire par un *Noli tangere matrem*' (Sade closes off the affair with a 'thou shalt not touch the mother').

> La mère reste interdite. Notre verdict est confirmé sur la soumission de Sade à la Loi. D'un traité vraiment du désir, peu donc ici, voire rien de fait. Ce qui s'en annonce dans ce travers pris d'une rencontre, n'est au plus qu'un ton de raison.
> (*FE*, 790)

[The mother remains forbidden. Our verdict is confirmed on the submission of Sade to the Law. As for a true treatise on desire, therefore, there's very little here, nothing in fact. What is announced of it in this back side of a meeting, is only at most a reasonable tone.]

In Kant, the subjectivity of form, of the Law of the Law, had depended on removing its object from all representation. In Sade only one (fundamental) object is denied such representation, denied the stage. Sade, Lacan writes, is perhaps more honest than Kant, who never designates the sexual (maternal?) nature of the object denied aesthetic form — the thing in itself.

The irony remains in both cases: dangling the object just out of reach of all transcendental aesthetic, sensual determination, veiling it, curtaining it off is what gives it all the more power, fascinating us, drawing us into metaphoric inference. Its outlines, Lacan writes, can be discerned as a 'bump' in the phenomenal veil: 'il ne manque d'apparaître à quelque bosse du voile phénoménal' (*FE*, 772).

Like the genitals, Lacan suggests that the curtaining of the object performed by 'form' is 'motivated' in Kant not so much as an exclusion of the mother as an averting of the gaze from the aim of the Other in demanding, commanding our sacrifice of pleasure to order. What must not be seen, what must not become the object of a perception, is the idea of the the Other's (God's) enjoyment:

> . . . Il ne faut pas que l'objet de la loi suggère une malignité du Dieu réel. Assurément le christianisme a éduqué les hommes à être peu regardants du côté de la jouissance de Dieu, et c'est en quoi Kant fait passer son volontarisme de la Loi-pour-la-Loi, lequel en remet, peut-on dire, sur l'ataraxie de l'expérience stoïcienne. On peut penser que Kant y est sous la pression de ce qu'il entend de trop près, non pas de Sade, mais de tel mystique de chez lui, en le soupir qui étouffe ce qu'il entrevoit au-delà d'avoir vue que son dieu est sans figure: *Grimmigkeit?* Sade dit: Etre-suprême-en-méchanceté.
>
> (*FE*, 773)

[. . . The object of the law must not suggest ill-will in the real God. Assuredly Christianity has educated men to look but little towards God's enjoyment, and it is that in which Kant has of his volontarism go from the Law-for-the-Law, which puts it back to the stoic experience. One might think that Kant is under the pressure of what he understands (hears) so closely, not of Sade, but of such and such a mystic from his home, in the sigh which stifles what he half sees beyond having seen that his God is without a figure (also face). *Grimmigkeit?* Sade says: Being-Supreme-in-Evil.]

Kant's effort was to de-ontologise, to keep the symbolic, the principle, content-free and outside of all particular arrangements by excluding the phenomenal, positive representation of the Good as a means to happiness. In Lacan this amounts to an embarrassed glance away from the enjoyment the gods derive from denying us ours. Eliminating the phenomenal is not a rule, but a self-imposed blindness. Kant's symbolic forms in no way succeed in reducing the symbolic to a pure ordering programme. Pretending that to impersonalise the Other as the It will break the pleasure principle still leaves intact the (third) person-al structure of this Order. Nothing prevents 'the symbolic' from becoming 'the support of that which was made into God'

(Mitchell, 153). In *Kant avec Sade* what is left out does not cease to operate as a power; and even though there is no positive depiction of the reward (happiness) for obedience to the laws of the order (being good) that does not prevent us from inferring a being to whom we deliver over our powers of enjoyment. And if 'It' is no longer the benign, fatherly 'Good old God of all times', after Kant, if Its 'joy' is not a joy in Goodness, then it can only be a joy in Evil. 'God' henceforth is, possibly, malignant, but It enjoys.

> *Kraft durch Freud* (strength through joy) there's a laugh for you. . . . There is a morality — that is the inference — of sexual conduct. The morality of sexual conduct is implicit in everything that has ever been said about the Good. Only, by having good to say, you end up with Kant, where morality admits to what it is. This is something which I felt needed to be argued in an article *Kant with Sade* — morality admits it is Sade.
>
> (Mitchell, 157–8)

The Enjoyment of The Other

For Lacan it is not simply the sequence of first the displacement of reality by the image, and then the 'murder of the thing' by the word, that constitutes the dimension of the radically new — Symbolic — order in the interhuman circuit. Taking again the image of the Saussurian couple, speaker and listener, we need to understand specifically how the word is *given*, and why this opens the symbolic, the wound.

The word is given to the other, whose ears pick it up and whose mouth is supposed to give it back in a reciprocal act of exchange. But the reciprocity of exchange, the 'line by which two subjects are supposed to be linked in a situation of reversibility and equality' is interrupted already by the fact of the voice and enunciation. Any word that is given and which expects reciprocity already calls on a third party or witness, tacitly, that the return will be made. Lacan used the image of a depositor, in *Kant avec Sade* (*FE*, 767) who gives something to another to keep for him and to be returned at a later date, on the basis of a mutual trust. One deposits desires, one's libidinal 'energy', with the Other.

146

A gift to the moral order, even if it is no longer in the form of a community, a culture, an aggregation of human beings, but a mere set of forms, is still, Lacan finds, a diverted desire, a diverted libido. Sexual energy is still what *drives* even the Symbolic Order. With Kant, the Order arrives at its 'purest' (most detached and abstract) form, but one nevertheless dependent on a certain empirical experience: hearing. At the minimum, the drive of the symbolic order can be reduced to the structure of the 'splitting of the subject' by the fact of the laws of speech, separating the 'sujet de l'énoncé' and the 'sujet de l'énonciation':

> On apperçoit ici tout nûment se reveler se à quoi nous intro-duirait la parodie plus haut donnée de l'universel évident du devoir du dépositaire, à savoir que la bipolarité dont s'instaure la Loi morale n'est rien d'autre que cette refente du sujet s'opère de toute intervention du signifiant: nommément du sujet de l'énonciation au sujet de l'énoncé. La Loi morale n'a pas d'autre principe.
>
> (*FE*, 770)

(One sees quite nakedly revealed here that to which we intro-duced above the parody of the universal evident in the duty of the depositor, to wit that the bipolarity by which the Law is instituted is none other than this splitting of the subject which is operated by every intervention of the signifier: namely of the subject of the enunciation from the subject of the enunciated. Moral law has no other principle.)

Obedience to the law of the return is based on a moral maxim that can only be offered equally in the form of the voice. In fact, the word excludes all reciprocity, and all systems of morality based on reciprocity. The word is given not just to another subject, it is also addressed to a third party as witness: the Other. Any appeal to the reciprocity of another calls forth, calls on and invokes, inevitably, the Other. As *given*, as voiced, the recipro-cal word implies a moral maxim that one prescribes freely to oneself, appearing in the form of a voice of Otherness, coming from Elsewhere.

The Symbolic Order requires transcending initial 'exchange':

how would the third party exist if not for the first two? 'He' and 'she' appear only in the exchange of words between 'I' and 'you'. Imperatives are always in the form of the sentence. The voice that speaks is also heard, not just by the addressee, but by the self that speaks it. The subject who speaks, who says 'I', for example, already designates a split between the ego and the subject (who can never be in the same place and at the same time as the signifier (I) that marks its place).

The two Kantian imperatives of (1) excluding reciprocity between subjects, and (2) remaining indifferent to content (bureaucratic ideals, really) along with the rejection of *pathos* allow Kant to liberate the moral field. But they also provide the energy required for driving the (a)moral order. Not a set of fixed categories, but a constant displacement and substitution of the object of desire motivates the subject of the Symbolic Order. The liberation Kant desires, the liberation from the personal and intersubjective must, unfortunately, be announced; the maxim must be uttered. And its phenomenal form reveals the latent intersubjectivity in Kant's project: the belief in the Order as an Other. What Lacan finds is that the entire moral project would fail without the form of a *particular kind of maxim*, the promise of fidelity, of being true to one's word. This maxim alone is the symbolic paradigm or prototype of all ethical law in Kant (the self-identical word that gives itself voice, the law that must be obeyed — freely).

In the end, morality and amorality are, for Lacan, the same: speech, even in the form of the moral maxim attempting to be a pure form of freedom, opens the field of the Other and deposits in it all pleasure, all joy. What Lacan is suggesting is that the 'universal moral law' begins to founder on the suggestion that a will and a pleasure lies 'within' the Law, within the 'Other'. That the moral order itself is what has rights over our enjoyment, keeps us as much '*à la botte*' as the discourse of unmoved Being and Goodness ever did. We are made to serve the desire and the enjoyment of the Other.

What happens is that, through the act of speech, all the freedom (in Sade's case, his maxim is his freedom to enjoy — the body of another) must be given over exclusively to the Other, thereby rendering It the sole being who enjoys. Only the Other can break the circle of pleasure and guarantee one's freedom from its bindings; but the consequence is that all power of enjoyment — in the sexual and possessive senses the French term *jouir* has — is located in the Law of the Law, freely willed, self-imposed restraints, restrictions and negations. No one but the Order, the Other, has the right to enjoy.

This radical inversion powers the *drive* of the Symbolic Order. Kant taboos the object; by placing Kant side by side with Sade, Lacan suggests a sexual implication to this taboo. Sade, at the limit of the intersubjective circle, just at the edge where the subject remains a subject and can suffer pain and pleasure, still has the alibi of immortality (in the form of the threat of Hell) to keep his work on this side of the radicalness of Kant. The refusal of the aim of happiness — the total exclusion of pleasure, the death of desire — as constitutive of the Law in Kant opens a way to moving beyond the intersubjective circle and into the Symbolic. This order depends on exclusions, the exclusion of the meaning of the sexual relation, and it operates as the unconscious, driven by the signifier.

Driving around in the Symbolic Order

I have argued that most readers of Lacan have de-emphasised his specifying and characterising of the positive mode in which the incest taboo, the sacrifice is offered in modern civilisation. Every law is the repression of a desire, but we must ask, at what point does this repression generalise, accelerate, create a society of Laws, not men? Modern society is characterised specifically by the absence of a fixed set of categories, of prescriptions and proscriptions for desire, as in a kinship system of tabooed sexual objects. Desire as such is not recognised by the Law, which in effect renders it unconscious in the technical sense.

Lacan, in his reading of Freud along culture-critical lines, saw in the absence of fixed categories a masking of the cultural Drive. The drive of the Symbolic is a drive to break up 'natural' and conscious relationships and reorganise them purely symbolically, recombining them purely according to the principles without regard for their content. What we have failed to notice, is that that 'principle' has a very particular form, the rhetorical one of metaphor, carried to a higher power, abstracted to the level of values beyond worth,[16] the form of negation-in-the-mode-of-free-choice. And in the new, the economical order, it cannot remain anchored or attached to meaning. It must be content-free, able to move on to symbolise, mediate and render unconscious any social arrangement, any particular economic order.

What Lacan sees in modern culture is not a lessening but a heightening of the drive to sacrifice — not to the promise of pleasure, of satisfaction — the 'eternal feminine no longer calls from on high' — but to the *dark god*, the malevolent god the Nazis worshipped.

Kant accomplished the most important cultural disconnection — the final divorce between the moral imperative and the promise of a reward of 'Happiness' for one's submissive 'Goodness'. Lest one think, however, that the historic obedience to the imperatives of the Superego on the strength of the promise of compensation for one's sacrifice of libidinal energy to cultural duty falters with the loss of faith in civilisation as ultimate Good, fading along with Kant's demolition of eudaemonism, we need only note that this is far from certain: the liberation of the libido from cultural constraints is hardly accomplished by this divorce; rather, quite extraordinarily, it appears all the more tightly bound. If the 'Symbolic' is the 'support of that which was made into God' it does not necessarily follow that the supposed 'death of God' deconstructs the system of constraints, the diversion of libido.

For Lacan, Kant and his critique of the ideological aim of 'Goodness' from whose endpoint all moments could be evaluated for their systemic 'place', constitute a turning-point in cultural history. His deconstruction of a phenomenalising of the demands of the symbolic as a moral order offered a latent critique of the metaphoric process of culture formation. Yet, because he failed to criticise in his own work the phenomenal mode in which he himself understood/heard the moral law Kant's thought did not prevent us from continuing to drive on down the superhighways, the *'grand'routes'*, of metaphoric culture. It may have actually helped us along the way.

For if the symbol is 'above' the phenomenon, moving in the direction of — but never reaching — the universal, its power derives from the absence of its object, an absence which drives us towards it. Kant himself thus appears as a crossroads. He de-ontologised form, and pointed us towards it as an activity that produced the aura of being. But by cutting off the object of the Law he did not do away with the desire for that lost object, he merely rendered our desire for it *unconscious*. In curtaining the object, Kant made it continue to be the support of that which was made into God; he did not prevent our conceiving the Symbolic Order as a set of messages or signs from the Other, who loves us and to whom we sacrifice all our libidinal energy, all our power to enjoy. The partitioned object becomes the '*objet a*', which we imagine as a sign of the Other, a 'reflection of like to like'. It is Lacan's self-imposed task to divorce the *objet a* from the imaginary and narcissistic 'love' relationship — which is simply another way of accomplishing his even more central task, that of reminding us that the drive of culture is neither benevolent nor malevolent; it is a mindless, inexorable drive towards division, splitting. It is aimed, but only at pro-ducing, through this fission, the energy and the power to perpetuate itself.

Notes

1. See Mary Douglas's *Purity and Danger* (London, Routledge and Kegan Paul, 1969); Everett C. Hughes, 'Good People and Dirty Work', in *The Sociological Eye; Selected Papers on Institutions and Race* (Chicago and New York, Aldine/Atherton, 1971), pp. 87–97; and Julia Kristeva, *Powers of Horror: An Essay on Abjection* (New York, Columbia University Press, 1982).
2. See Dean and Juliet MacCannell's study of the feminine beauty guidebooks, in N. Armstrong and L. Tennenhouse, *The Ideology of Conduct*, Methuen Books, forthcoming; Robin Tolmach Lakoff and Raquel L. Scherr, *Face Value: The Politics of Beauty* (Boston, London, Melbourne and Henley, Routledge and Kegan Paul, 1984), and Rita J. Freedman, *Beauty Bound* (Lexington, Mass., Lexington Books/D.C. Heath, 1986).
3. Anthony Wilden examines the Lévi-Straussian/McLuhanesque opposition of 'hot' and 'cold' societies from the point of view of their relationship to *memory* in *System and Structure*, 407–12.
4. 'Cover-up' is the precise term here: whether it takes the societal form of covering the genitals or the religious mode of veiling the sacred, it is the act of covering which mobilises civilisation's energies. Even

when a Heidegger or a Freud can show that the important thing to be covered is a no-thing ('truth', the 'woman' in the castration complex) the structure remains the same. Lacan seems to me to have pointed the way to Derrida's questioning of this structure.

5. A geometry of nuclear fission? Taken in another iconic frame, the Borromean knot looks like the symbol of the atom ⊗.

6. It is no accident that Lacan's critics have focused his work on the Symbolic Order as his outstanding contribution to his field. But there is almost no agreement either as to what he is saying about it, nor about his own attitude towards, or evaluation of, it.

His most important reader, Jacques Derrida, has taken off from Lacan's same starting-point, seeing the Symbolic Order as a *code* conceived along semiotic lines, Derrida's critique is that only a certain version of the semiotic dominates even Lacan's assumptions about how the code as a mechanism of value-creation operates. In the *Grammatology*, Derrida's argument runs that the model for the code as an interplay of positive and negative, of presence and absence, is a model unaware of its restriction to the phonological analysis of the word. By restricting the analysis of the word to the paradigmatic, an oppositional notion of value-creation is emphasised at the expense of the connective or syntagmatic. Both paradigm and syntagm are revalued in the context of the 'other scene' of language, the synchronic, *langue*. Overemphasising the dimension of the *parole* as value-creation from an analytic viewpoint merely repeats rather than resists the way culture operates to oppose *meaning*. It is therefore crucial, in Derrida's practice, to deal with the *semantic* in such a way that, as Lacan puts it, 'all its *uses* are added up', so that something like the (interhuman) meaning, cancelled by signification, is able to be thought.

That we have a bias in favour of the phonic, the voice, etc. is as much the heart of Lacan's critique of the Other as Derrida's; the major difference between the two is that Derrida wishes not only to lay bare our subjection to the word, but to reframe and recast the way we 'think' the code governing signification. 'Before' opposition and identity he would see mere *difference* pre-positioning the phonologic play of presence and absence. In *'différence'*, the Other would have found its Other. Thus, in its aims Derrida's 'mastery' of the code seems to me to be in line with Lacan's discovery of *intelligent (interlineal) reading* as a way of 'reading elsewhere than the way the symbolic is written' (*Ornicar?*, 1975, 91).

The Derrida–Lacan relationship is a complex one, and since Lacan on occasion commented on Derrida in his last years, it would need a patient scholar to track it. There can be no doubt that Lacan's work was highly suggestive for Derrida, who has continued to follow up the terms Lacan seemed most fascinated by — not only the word, the voice, reading, the sun, the centre, but also the ear — and with the same concern for the forms of social ties — ideologically concretised as institutions — that these figures, replacing the body, have made and are making. I want to indicate here how powerfully Lacan's fingering of code and its appearance and hiding as the Other and the It has effected a certain direction for at least one of the most radical of modern thinkers.

7. See Paul de Man, 'Semiology and Rhetoric', in *Allegories of Reading*; and my essay, 'The Temporality of Textuality: Bahktin and Derrida', *op. cit.*

8. See my remarks in 'Oedipus Wrecks', pp. 911–12.

9. *Scilicet* 6/7 (1975), 37, where Lacan calls *Verwerfung* 'the judgement which chooses and rejects', distinguished from *Verneinung*, the denial that is a mode attempting, but failing, to exorcise the truth.

10. 'Visual Pleasure and Narrative Cinema', *Screen* 16 (Autumn 1975), pp. 6–7.

11. A wonderful illustration of the fragmenting and explosive quality of the male look, modelled on the castrating and dividing power of the Other appears in Marguérite Duras's *La Maladie de la mort* (Paris, Editions de Minuit, 1982) tr. in English in the *Evergreen Review*, 98 (1984), 79–90. Duras employs a narrative voice, which is clearly not the implied masculine one of traditional narrative, that minutely details, in the mode of an address to him, what a man is thinking and feeling about the woman he has hired to make love to him. Duras's text has the woman looking back and asking questions of the man, asking the Freudian question, *Was will das Weib?*, in reverse:

Et puis elle demande: Vous voulez quoi?
Vous dites que vous voulez essayer, tenter la chose, tenter connaître ça, vous habituer à ça, à ce corps, à ces seins, à ce parfum, à la beauté, à ce danger de mise au monde d'enfants que représente ce corps, à cette forme imberbe sans accidents musculaires ni de force, à ce visage, à cette coïncidence entre cette peau et la vie qu'elle recouvre. (8)

[And then she asks: What is that you want?
You say that you want to try, to feel the thing, to know that, to get accustomed to it, to this body, to these breasts, to this fragrance, to beauty, to this danger of childbirth which this body represents, to this hairless form neither rough nor sinewy, to this face, to this bare skin, to this meeting here of this skin and the life which covers it. (79)]

The description, in disjointed pieces, of 'masculine desire' contrasts with Duras's later description of the woman, who looks at the man and is told to shut her eyes and her mouth:

Vous regardez encore. Le visage est laissé au sommeil, il est muet, il dort comme les mains. Mais toujours l'esprit affleure à la surface du corps, il le parcourt tout entier, et de telle sorte que chacune des parties de ce corps témoigne à elle seule de sa totalité, la main comme les yeux, le bombement du ventre comme le visage, les seins comme le sexe, les jambes comme les bras, la respiration, le coeur, les tempes, les tempes comme le temps. (27)

[You look again. The face remains asleep, it is mute, it sleeps like the hands. But, always, the mind comes to the surface of the body, journeys through it, and this in such a way that each of the parts of this body bears witness, singly, to the whole of it, the hands as well as the eyes, the bulge of the loins as well as the face, the breasts as well as the sex, the legs as well as the arms, the respiration, the heart, the temples as well as time. (83)]

12. I think, in contrast to Kristeva's neo-romanticism, of James's *Maisie*, who inserts her desire *between* language codes, expressing her desire (to stay with her stepfather, without all the pseudo-mothers in her life) in *franglais* (Henry James, *What Maisie Knew*, Harmondsworth, Middlesex, Penguin Books, 1984, p. 236). See my *Couplings: The Failures of Heterosexuality from Rousseau to Lacan* (the Johns Hopkins University Press, in preparation). I have written elsewhere, in 'Oedipus Wrecks', of the need to inhabit the house of culture differently, slipping between its rooms. Derrida writes of hymens; Lacan insists on ambiguities.

13. For Lacan, the human subject explodes when its glance is turned back on itself (*II*, xv, 208). What makes this explosion, this fission, is the presence (= absence) of the Other: 'What structures the gaze is what is not there' (*I*, xviii, 249). If knowledge of one's being is linked to the ego sphere, then this third party, who is 'supposed to know', can only be inferred on the model of the ego. But the ego is also related to others: it is the particular definition of how it relates to this other that Lacan wants to reform.

14. This 'principle' is mathematically expressed as the division of nothing (read: the human, speaking being) by Nothing (the Symbolic Order) equals infinity ∞ (which looks a lot like Lacan's Moebius strips) Lacan writes about zero:

Everyone knows that if zero appears in the denominator the value of the fraction no longer has meaning, but assumes by convention what mathematicians call infinite value. In a way this is one of the stages in the constitution of the subject. In so far as the primary signifier is pure non-sense, it becomes the bearer of the infinitisation of the value of the subject, not open to all meanings, but abolishing them all, which is different. (*4FC*, 252)

15. Given Clément's belief in the importance of aesthetic distance (77), one can understand this (hopeful) reading of Kant in relation to Sade.

16. See above, chapter on Metaphor and Value.

7

Powering the Cultural Drive

The objective of my teaching, in as much as it aims at the part of analytic discourse which can be formulated, or put down, is to dissociate the a and the O by reducing the former to what belongs to the imaginary and the latter to what belongs to the symbolic. That the symbolic is the support of that which was made into God is beyond doubt. That the imaginary is supported by the reflection of like to like, is certain. And yet, a has come to be confused with the S(O) beneath which it is written on the board, and it has done so under pressure of the function of being. It is here that a rupture or severance is needed.

(Lacan, 'A Love Letter' (Mitchell, 153–4))

Let us say that the domain of sexuality shows a natural functioning of signs. At this level they are not signifiers, for the nervous (illness) is a symptom, and according to the definition of the sign, something intended for someone. The signifier, being something quite different, represents a subject for another signifier.

(Lacan, *Four Fundamental Concepts* (157))

Culture: The Unconscious Scene of Metaphor

There can be no doubt as to Lacan's role in having underscored the unconscious for psychoanalysis, as he adopted the role of gadfly to a profession that had become partisans of the ego over the unconscious — an ego which, far from resisting being split by culture, responds to its mutilation by a 'higher' order with love. Lacan reminded the analysts that this love-ideology, the relationship of identification between culture and the ego, is more devastating than the splitting itself, which installs culture with its benefits and drawbacks. The disruption of this identification is crucially important to Lacan. This is why the Freudian unconscious had been such an important, critical discovery. In a world more and more subjected to the imperatives

155

of order, the Freudian unconscious — when it slips — alleviates the splitting of the person, momentarily derails the drive. Thus Lacan insists to the analysts on the supreme importance of the unconscious.

But, as I have read Lacan, for him, the Freudian, the deep, unknown knowledge of a desired but forbidden relationship, is not the only unconscious. The critical disagreement among his readers as to how Lacan evaluated the unconscious and its role in human history is due to his linking the Symbolic with one kind of unconscious. As *an* unconscious, the Symbolic Order is the locus not of the moderation but the deepening of alienation and dispossession. In the *Ecrits* Lacan hints that the structure of desire is that of alienation; in the *Seminars* he explicitly defines desire as alienation. The unconscious of alienated desire is the place of primary and secondary repression, where the narcissistic ego-istic version of the self, sees, hears and subjects itself to its own repressed desires in inverted form.

For Lacan, then, there are two possible versions of the unconscious. The one unconscious, the one of which Freud dreams, is one that we, as speaking, cultured beings have never (yet) experienced. It is the scene of a fictional and retrospective nostalgia for a time and place outside metaphoric enclosures, for language as a neutral 'third term' or common ground that would allow the possibility of the mutual co-recognition of desire between two selves. It is a scene 'before' the loss of the mutuality of desire, of being together for the sake of pleasure. It is, of course, a scene which may never yet have existed in human history, an interstitial moment between the two extremes of savage and civilised individuality and separateness. That which *could have been between* human beings — familial *eros*, the sheer pleasures of association (as Rousseau's discourse on inequality puts it, people associate because they happen to be nearby and it gives them pleasure) — is always prevented (in the etymological sense also of 'coming before') by the cultural drive: the drive to organise, to regularise. The drive allows the human being to associate with the other only if he does so according to symbolic rules, or negative terms for order, the incest taboo primarily.

The other unconscious is that of the fall into alienated desire. Here the means for linking two selves in a common enterprise, the 'common ground' of language, or the sign, develops a *formal relation*, a *moral law* that rules what takes place between the two. It — formal rules, grammar, Law — diverts libidinal interest away from the co-participants, becoming not merely a means of communication, but a fundamental code. It will become the guarantor of the trust, the authenticity, and ultimately the being of those who converse with each other. This 'unconscious' — the It, the code — comes to be much more than a neutral meeting-place, a common ground: It becomes a final Court of Appeal, a Judge, a Subject, the Other. Ultimately it is the site of the *truth* which, as Lacan writes, 'is based only on the fact that speech, even when it consists of lies, appeals to it, gives rise to it', (*4FC*, 133).

Transformed into a *moral* law, 'which looked at more closely, is simply desire in its pure state, that very desire that culminates in the sacrifice, strictly speaking, of everything that is the object of love in one's human tenderness' (*4FC*, 275), it regulates and rules the relationship between self and other — or, rather, of non-relationship. Its commands are always negative, its structure that of separating the sexes, and denying mutually recognised desire.

It is, in short, the *basis* of civilisation.

So much so, that, from within the boundaries of culture, we find any other mode of existence almost inconceivable. If simple, mutually recognised desires ever existed they always already contained the seeds of their own destruction: speech is already language, code. We know that in no matter what version we have the history of culture — Rousseau's *Second Discourse* or Freud's *Jenseits*, for example — the apparently simple desire for pleasure necessarily becomes a complex *principle*: repetition, habit, the compulsion to repeat and to organise and shape any stray, wild or contingent ('natural') associations definitively supplants/supplements any so-called 'first' form of human association.

But let us try, nevertheless, to see the positive attraction of the other, 'uncivilised' scene, even though we have negatively mythified it. The 'first' scene *attracts* us if only by virtue of its being opposed to the alternative, symbolic, civilised scene: the scene of alienation, order and negation — the scene of *culture*.

Inside culture's boundaries, the 'first' scene is relegated to the unconscious.[1] Lacan writes that the psychotic, for example, cannot leave it behind and exchange it for a proper place in the symbolic order. He stays (in his heart) with 'the family' as it is staged for him in just such a 'first' scene. The psychotic subject suffers from an 'inertia', Lacan writes, that makes him 'speak only of papa or mama' (*Scilicet*, 6/7, 1976, 44–5). By speaking 'only of papa or mama' the psychotic is actually opposing the *polis* (*la cité*): for Lacan the private family framed in 'this other scene', this *andere Schauplatz* is a form of (political as well as personal) opposition to civil society.

The psychotic may be the last person in our society to dream immoral dreams; and Lacan is clearly not advocating the primacy of psychosis. Yet it is important to inquire into the structure of desire in the other scene, in the unconscious that resists culture. Interestingly, when we look at it through Lacan, we find it equally dominated by a linguistic figure — metonymy.[2] We do not, as one might expect, find pre-civil desire outside language; but we do find it coded *differently*, with a different accent, tone, and gender form.

Metaphor and Metonymy in the Two Scenes of the Unconscious

The metonymic mode is characterised by Lacan as the mode of *desire*, or desire in a mode that runs counter to the modality of desire as alienation, metaphoric desire. In the (unconscious) scene where the *metonymic* dominates we have a combinatory, associative mode; in the scene dominated by metaphor, we have splitting and disconnection, covered up by an illusion of unity and wholeness.

In each of the two different scenes, the alternative trope is decentred and devalued: in the cultural economy metonymy, real connection, is seen as retrogressive, inefficient, un(re)productive, an unnecessary doubling and expenditure of energy. Metaphor is valued as a binding and a control of the free libidinal energy because it gives a way of offering this surplus as a sacrificial gift to the Other. It is also, Lacan writes, 'satisfying', but not in the mode of satisfying the body, sexual reality.

Sublimation is . . . the satisfaction of the drive, without repression. In other words — for the moment, I am not fucking, I am talking to you. Well! I can have exactly the same satisfaction as if I were fucking. That's what it means. Indeed, it raises the question of whether in fact I am not fucking at this moment. . . It is clear that those with whom we deal, the patients, are not satisfied, as one says, with what they are. And yet, we know that everything they experience, even their symptoms, involves satisfaction. They satisfy something that no doubt runs counter to that with which they might be satisfied, or rather, perhaps, they give satisfaction *to* something. They are not content with their state, but all the same, being in a state that gives so little content, they are content. The whole question boils down to the following — *what* is contented here? On the whole. . . . I would say that to which they give satisfaction by the ways of displeasure is nevertheless . . . the law of pleasure . . . What we have before us in analysis is a system in which everything turns out all right, and which attains its own sort of satisfaction.

(*4FC*, 165–6)

Metaphor is the means by which we 'ethically' deliver sexuality up *to* the drive, to the 'law of pleasure', pleasure regulated by a rule, a principle. An only apparently erotic drive, it is death alone that the pleasure principle implies, relentlessly signifies, the link between sex and death: 'the link between sex and death, sex and death of the individual is fundamental' (*4FC*, 150).

'Violence is originary with language', Derrida, in Lacan's wake, writes (*Gramm.*, 108–9) telling us of the 'irreducibility of metaphor, the irremediable absence of the proper name'. At the same time 'obliteration constitutes the legibility of what it erases'. The elevation and cancellation of the individual through the signifier of reproduction — metaphor, paternity, Lacan's *Booz* — is a story of the life given over to 'civilisation' to the species at the expense of the death of the individual: what cannot be borne, in the discourse it legislates, is the generic, the collective, the 'more than one' that sexuality would force us to have us 'think'. In other words, the death of the individual can be mourned when it is metaphorised, and sacrificed to a greater Individual — the collective Order; but metonymised, it can be seen as a retrieval of connection, a loss of isolation.

If Lacan's work suggests, as I have argued, the constant critique of one-ness and individualism — the ideological forms of the 'one' which create the 'Other' — then, the death of the individual, that 'element' ('element: "1",': for Lacan it is a 'unitary trait', a 'feature', *'sa'*: *Ornicar?* 11, 1977, 4) so stubbornly defended by Aristotle against all generality, the 'death' of the individual need not be such a tragedy.

> Existence, thanks to sexual division, rests upon copulation, accentuated in two poles that time-honoured tradition has tried to characterise as the male pole and the female pole. This is because the mainspring of reproduction is to be found there. Around this fundamental reality, there have always been grouped, harmonised, other characteristics, more or less bound up with the finality of reproduction. . . . We know today how, in society, a whole distribution of functions in a play of alternation is grounded on this terrain. It is modern structuralism that has brought this out best, by showing that it is at the level of matrimonial alliance, as opposed to natural generation, to biological lineal descent — at the level therefore of the signifier — that the fundamental exchanges take place and it is there that we find once again that the most elementary structures are inscribed in terms of a combinatory. The integration of this combinatory into sexual reality raises the question of whether it is not in this way that the signifier came in to the world, into the world of man.
>
> (*4FC*, 150–1)

'From the fact of making one, there substitution begins', Lacan teaches his seminar students — this time Americans — the 'origin' of metaphor (*Ornicar?* 11, 1977, 4). It is also the 'origin' of culture: 'The characteristic of elements is that one proceeds to their combination.' Culture reduces two to one and then recombines them according to its principles, its laws. The reduction of the two forms metaphor/metonymy to one is not only an example but *the* mechanism of the production of culture, just as is the conflation of the symbolic and the anti-symbolic unconscious in the dream. If, that is, it ever really does 'combine'. For when human sexuality as reproduction is seen as a 'combinatory' through the signifier, and therefore through metaphor, it can only 'operate, at certain of its stages, by the expulsion of a remainder' (*4FC*, 151): by means, that is, of negation, the 'selective' side of metaphor on which 'combination' depends.

The Remainder and the Drive

It is this 'remainder', this leftover, what has 'fallen' away from the shaping of human reproduction that Lacan will call the *objet petit a*, and it is around this remainder that all of Lacan's analytic interventions will be offered. For it is the *way* in which we treat the 'remainder' that will determine whether we can break the relationship, the narcissistic relationship, of 'the one to the Other', that is the source of our misery. Lacan writes, 'If the Other is taken away man cannot sustain the position of Narcissus' (EE, 195) and that

> The objective of my teaching, in as much as it aims at that part of analytic discourse which can be formulated, or put down, is to dissociate the *a* and the *O*, by reducing the former to what belongs to the imaginary and the latter to what belongs to the symbolic. That the symbolic is the support of that which was made into God is beyond doubt.
>
> (Mitchell, 153–4)

The 'combinatory' of human sexuality is cultural, economic: ruled by a 'bipolarity' that, in the oppositional mode shaped by metaphor, is reduced to a single element. The final phrase of the quote on sexual division from *4FC* (150–1) above contains two of the words Lacan loaded most heavily with the significance of the culturally oppressive: 'man' and 'world'. Finally, what metaphor fathers is only the Other, who promises much but offers literally nothing in the combinatory mode — *'amour'*, *'être père'*, *'faire un'*. Its law, its drive is the prevention of natural, necessary and pleasurable combinations.

Metaphor powers as well as empowers: unchecked by metonymy, unresisted by irony, unremarked, it will 'drive on', demanding sacrifice after sacrifice until Nothing remains without remainder. The drive in Lacan is the law of a return, the

161

overshooting of the aim and its redounding on the head of the one who desires. For Lacan, it is the deconstruction of the drive that is the aim of analysis, to be effected through the transference.

The drive is powered by an accelerating metaphorical fission, a splitting of the atoms of human life, by the 'sacrifice' culture imposes as its due (communal gain or profit) in exchange for the comforts and satisfactions it promises. Self is divided from other by the alienation work of desire and language. Disconnection of the self from the other draws off libidinal energy for the work of civilisation. That is the first stage. Yet another, supplementary, excess (or surplus) of energy is gained by the alienation or splitting of the subject (the ego — ego-ideal division). The drive gathers momentum until it divides all entities according to conceptual principles, while operating as a (pseudo)unifying force.

In fact there is no such thing as 'the' drive for Lacan, but only partial drives, since the key element is always left out of its representation, the reproductive act:

> [N]o drive represents . . . the totality of the *Sexualstrebung* . . . as it might be conceived as making present in the psyche the function of *Fortpflänzung*, of reproduction, if this function entered the psyche at all . . . This function is not represented as such in the psyche.
>
> *(4FC*, 204)

In the psyche, only the *equivalents* of the reproductive function appear, in the form of principles of polarity — negative/ positive, active/passive, etc. The 'drive' is partial because it is attached to only one of these poles — the active, or 'masculine' one. It is this symbolic arrangement alone,

> only this division . . . that makes necessary . . . that the ways of what one must do as man or as woman are entirely abandoned to the drama, to the scenario, which is placed in the field of the Other — which, strictly speaking, is the Oedipus complex.
>
> *(4FC*, 204)

The double scene is reduced to a single arena, the field of the

Other, or the play of signifiers in which only the symbolic ordering of the sexual relation can be admitted.

Lacan distinguishes the drive absolutely from instinct: 'nous manquons tout à fair à l'instinct', he tells his MIT audience in 1977. For Lacan the definition of the drive given in Freud's metapsychological writings shows that its aim is a new order from that which had powered the 'first' deployment of culture: it is not simply from the satisfaction of a need that the drive arises, but a positive thrust away from satisfaction, away from the sexual relation and into the symbolic, disconnected one. Literature since the end of the eighteenth century has told us this story repeatedly, about which more later.

If it is not-Satisfaction that drives culture, the disconnection of self and other, then this amounts to saying, as Lacan indeed does, that what *organises* the drive are finally negative sexual concepts. The one thing, he writes, that the psyche cannot admit is the sexual relation: only tokens, substitutes, stand-ins, concepts symbolising sexual reproduction are permitted (e.g. principles of activity, passivity, etc.: *4FC*, 204).

The power of the drive *depends* on the barring of the sexual relation from the psyche, on the prohibition of connexivity — except according to conceptual lines that preclude connection. The categorical imperative is that boundaries, distinctions must be maintained. Within the drive *'l'amour'* becomes for Lacan *'l'amur'*: the wall between the sexes.

How does the drive become operational, by what means do the imperatives, the moral imperatives of metaphoric culture — the imperatives to make distinctions covered by an ideological form of one-ness — actually affect the subject? We have, with Kant, already discovered the ear-god of the logocentric world of culture; with Lacan we also have the visual signifier, the little letter, to mark the presence of his Janus-face, the eye-ear-god.

The *Object* of the Drive: *le petit a*

When Lacan comments on psychoanalysis as both a science and distinct from a science, he does so on the basis of a prior distinction between science and Science. Science, capital S, is the Science of 'little letters', formalised, signified by means of letters that are not capitalised. Lacan writes of the difference between letters as simple material and letters as signifiers of something beyond — the 'spirit'. The letter seems to us to stand between us and its significance, its 'spirit'. And yet, Lacan asks, how would we ever get a 'spirit' without a letter?

Cartesian algebra is the first to disfigure the letter in the direction of the universal, free concept, by having subtracted from it any specified value. Lacan contrasts the Cartesian use of small letters with the Hebrew alphabet, in which the letters are all capitals, and also have a numerical value, that of a series, first, second, third. Descartes, the first to have attempted to divorce the letter from the tendency to make it significant (it is value-free and therefore open to all values, any value) is, ironically, the first subject to make its doubt about its place and value into a form of certainty, of determination. The disconnection of the algebraic letter from any signification whatsoever seems at first, then, an advance, an important deliverance from the mystification of meaning; but this is only an apparent triumph. Just as Descartes turned Montaigne's doubting, suspended, ambiguous consciouness into a mode of security and gave himself a foundation, so too, his 'little letters' did not escape the process of *signification*. Signifying — implying values beyond the phenomenal and material — is that process in which mere markings become signifiers, appealing to, calling on something, someone 'beyond' to validate them. The little letter comes to stand for something: Science itself, that which stands over and above the performance of scientific acts (*4FC*, 126 ff.). For Lacan, even the Cartesian algebraic letter comes to signify not a specific value (this always remains ambiguous), but a *seemingly* valuable discourse, 'scientific' discourse. Descartes aimed at certainty only, leaving 'knowledge' to others; but in giving up meaning, significance and knowledge for the certainty of the mark he is perhaps only repressing doubt, the doubt that the letter might signify something . . .

Playing Pascal to this Descartes, Lacan figures the ways in which the 'neutral', universal, algebraic, 'independent' symbol is always only a metaphor, a product not of a pure symbolic order and code, but also of the imaginary. The famous passage in the 'Agency of the Letter in the Unconscious', where he iterates the metaphorical cancellation of the tree by all the figurative trees of human cultural memory (EE, 154–5), demonstrates the failure of the concept to appear without the concourse of the imaginary.

> For even broken down into the double spectre of its vowels and consonants, it can still call up with the robur and the plane tree the significations it takes on, in the context of our flora, of strength and majesty. Drawing on all the symbolic contexts suggested in the Hebrew of the Bible, it erects on a barren hill the shadow of the cross. Then reduces to the capital Y, the sign of a dichotomy which, except for the illustration used by heraldry, would owe nothing to the tree however genealogical we may think it. Circulatory tree, tree of life of the cerebellum, tree of Saturn, tree of Diana, crystals formed in a tree struck by lightning, is it your figure that traces our destiny for us in the tortoise-shell cracked by the fire, or your lightning that causes that slow shift in the axis of being . . .

Our meticulous attempts to 'read' Lacan's algorithms are already undermined in advance by his insistence on the letter-as-imaginary. Jane Gallop's heroic struggle in her *Reading Lacan* to explicate the following formulae (EE, 164)

$$\frac{I}{f(S)s}$$
$$f(S \ldots S') = S(-)s$$
$$\text{and}$$
$$\frac{S'}{f(S)S} \cong S(+)s$$

points out one of the features of Lacan's 'ideographic' use of the 'little letter' since, she notes, the S (signifier) is 'always on top', in contrast to Saussure's formula (Gallop, 120). Her method of reading the formula is admirable and correct in so far as it pulls out the 'significance' of the letters beyond any abstract mathematical paradigm. But Professor Gallop then goes off in a lateral direction, worrying about all the proliferation of S's and depth psychology and leaves us still wondering what is significant about the significance of S always being on top? What the formulae are intended to do is to strike the imagination where it can be touched, where its 'grasp' of significance is made possible. When Lacan writes, 'The sign + between ( ) represents the crossing of the bar — and the constitutive value of this crossing for the emergence of signification' (EE, 164) he is summing up the process his discourse never ceased to be about: the ideological substitution of a faith in the additional surplus value that is derived from the act of deletion, subtraction. We submit to castration because we believe it gives us added, indeed infinite, value. '[I]f, turning the weapon of metonymy against the nostalgia that it serves, I refuse to seek any meaning beyond tautology, if in the name of 'war is war' and 'a penny is a penny' I decide to be only what I am, how ever here can I elude the obvious fact that I am in that very act?' (EE, 165). The Order hinges on a 'letter' — the *I* — whose purely negative determination must be experienced in the mode of absolute value.

The Little Letter a

The 'little letter' is analogous to — even at times described by Lacan as — the *objet petit a*. And, for Lacan, it is *the* point on which the *drive* turns, swerving from its first 'aim' (satisfaction), toward putting itself on the circular path of the signifier. For Lacan, the conceptual drive is inherent in the signifier.

The *drive*, for Lacan (*4FC*, 206), always overshoots its target, redounding on the subject himself. In the metapsychology Freud had distinguished between *aim* — satisfaction — and *object* — the means to satisfaction. With the advent of *desire*, or human alienation, the aim is definitively bracketed or deferred, so that all of the affective drive is displaced into the object. But the object, no longer a means but an end, never satisfies, becoming instead the source of repeated, futile (the acceleration of the drive) attempts to satisfy desire. The object as pseudo-aim, then, is also the source of the metaphoric drive towards substitutability: one thing is as good as another in attempting the impossible.

This object Lacan renames as the *'objet petit a'*. What is always at issue in culture boils down to the reception of the *petit a*: as the by-product or nuclear waste of metaphoric fission, which operated, we should remember, 'at certain of its stages, by the expulsion of a remainder' (*4FC*, 151), it is a *metonym*, a rejected connection. On the other hand, as a signifier, an incipient metaphor, it is the *objet a* of which Lacan speaks in *Télévision*: the part-object valued, given prestige, because it has 'fallen from Being', appearing in the gap, the hole made by the circle: the pupil of the eye, the mouth, any orifice will do.

Few of Lacan's readers (Catherine Clément is one exception; 99–101) discuss the *objet a* precisely because it is taken both ways. It is literally the switchpoint, the turning-point not only for the analytic cure, but for the power culture has over us — and our resistance to this power. Lacan asked that the term remain untranslated, perhaps to retain the suggestion of abjection that is one of its faces. It is as a part of the circularity of the relation to the Other, Oedipus' power to drive the culture machine through division and re-unification, that the *petit objet a* appears in Lacan's theory.

The object as the site of infinite substitutability (since it can never be the Real Thing) necessarily carries a negative value if it is compared to the sacred — hidden — value of values. When seen in the field of the Other, the object appears at that point where the alienating process of desire begins (the translation of satisfiable need into the insatiable demand for love), where the split between the ego-ideal and the ideal ego becomes definitive. In this gap, this split, this cut, the object appears not as a means to satisfaction, but as an obstacle to it. A 'good' object from the point of view of alienated desire because it blocks immediate satisfactions and raises the subject to the level of the Other; a 'bad' object from the point of view of the subject because it is not the Other's demanded love, but only one of the 'proofs of love'. It has 'come' from the Other, which also means that it has somehow fallen from the level of the Other, is a signifier of the subject's separation from the other. With the potential for becoming, nonetheless, a medium of exchange with the other.

The Transference: Separating the Demand for Love from the Drive

Love is a sign that we are changing discourses.

(Lacan, *XX*, ii, 21)

The only counter to the drive of the signifier is a process modelled on Lacan's version of *the transference*.[3]

Lacan found that the secret on which psychoanalysis had stumbled, the mechanism of the 'cure' through the transference, was fundamentally distorted by the narcissistic frame, the ego-culture in which it was made to operate.

Lacan says that the aim of the transference is to 'separate demand from the drive' (*4FC*, 273). The work of the transference is to revalue the *objet petit a* no longer as abject, fallen, a sign of separation and splitting, but as a new kind of connexivity (Mitchell, 153; also *Ornicar?*, 12, 1966, 120). Freud had already called the transference a 'false connection', indicating that the new love-object is not the old one, the character from the 'other' scene that cannot dwell peacefully in the field of the Other. But to take this term of 'falsity' without evaluation, it is important to see that what Freud is doing is radical indeed: making a connection where none is permitted.

For illustration let us turn to Freud's *Dora*,[4] the case of the girl in whom Freud first noticed the effects of the transference, although he noticed that with her, transference had failed. Of Dora, Lacan says that 'too late Freud told her that she was beginning to love him' (*I*, xix, 269). But the failure is not on Dora's part alone, it is situated by 'civilisation' and the sexual relation of Freud to Dora as well, a sexual relation barred by that civilisation.

The text of Dora, as critics have repeatedly pointed out, is full of odd reversals on the part of Freud, who uses this case to demonstrate — in his patient — the mechanism of the 'reversal of affect' (45). Feminists have rewritten this text repeatedly,[5] charging a distortion in Freud that he all too evidently leaves himself open to.

Freud is too defensive, for example, on the question of his discussing explicitly sexual situations with Dora. Insisting on his having, as a medical man, 'the rights of the gynaecologist' (23), he at the same time attempts to prove that, like the girl who reads Rousseau's *Julie*, the child is already corrupted (23). Why the 'moral' tone in a social context that is, like that of a text contemporary with it, Henry James's *Maisie* (which Neil Hertz has compared to *Dora*), itself the scene of decadence and infidelities abounding? The defensiveness (65) is, already, a symptom . . .

When his attractive young patient announces her sexual sophistication by revealing her knowledge of her father's (venereally caused) impotence as well as of the existence of his liaison with Frau K., she adds that she 'knows very well that there are other ways to obtain satisfaction'. Readers assume her reference is to cunnilingus, but Freud's immediate conclusion is that Dora is speaking obliquely of fellatio, which he vividly depicts as 'sucking at the male organ' (68) and deduces from this particular exchange Dora's own interest in, desire for, and denial of her desire for 'the male organ'. Coupled with Freud's barely disguised autobiographical musings (in an aside) about the originally homosexual tendency of all desire, the misreading of Dora is abundantly evident. But why? Why does Freud leave himself open? Why so many obvious failures, which are so many obvious signs, for him, of sexuality? Perhaps the Freud who is *mise en scène* here yields to another Freud, who 'knows' — nothing, but also everything.

Consider *the situation of the analysis* (something Lacan never failed to consider). There is Dora, an attractive young women (and it is Freud who tells us of her attractiveness), lying on a couch in a semi-darkened room *alone* with a mature and sexually knowledgeable man, Freud, who cannot or will not 'touch her'. In this situation, Freud 'proves' that Dora loves him as a man, including everything that stands for him as a man (the male organ) and that he, as a man, stands for (including *'hommo-sexualité'*). This 'proof' of Dora's passion for him is a proof by 'signifiers': only when, Lacan writes, 'the signifier isn't functioning do we read the sign' (*III*, xxiii, 329). What Freud can only be revealing, of course, is that it is *he* who loves her. More importantly, what he is also proving — demonstrating with his very being — is the law of separation of the sexes, the failure of heterosexuality, the law of Oedipus and of civilisation. Freud is, of course, too 'civilised' to touch her.

And so he dreams of a Dora who would love him: demanding of her, 'Wouldn't you like to give me a little kiss just now?', a question which purportedly is an 'insight' into her repressed desire, but is also a traditional question asked by the one who desires to be kissed.

The *objet petit a* — the little thing, the penis — is *almost* revalued by this transference, this connection that is *almost* made. The penis is almost retrieved from the phallic, the meta-phoric drive, disrupted by Freud's love for Dora — 'outside the limits of the law, where alone it may live' as Lacan put it (*4FC*, 276). Not quite, because the confession of the love, verbalised, shows the inversion of the grammatical pronoun in the discourse of love, that Freud himself demonstrated to be the grammar of love: 'Wouldn't *you* like to kiss *me*', translated as 'I want to kiss you'. 'Too late,' Lacan writes, 'Freud told Dora that she loved him,'[6] which can only be read, knowing Lacan's knowledge of the inverse love grammar, the mask of ideology, 'that he loved her'.

The literary examples of this 'drive' are multiple; since the end of the eighteenth century — and often very much in the wake of Kant — they have proliferated. Exemplary of those writers who sensed the acceleration of the drive is the Prussian author, Heinrich von Kleist, who suffered as we know, a 'Kant-crisis', bitterly forsaking, after having read Kant, the eudaemonism and moral optimism of his early Leibnizian years. Kleist's works are full of the 'Freudian' unconscious, the sexual one, but they are equally full of intimations of the kind of 'drive' Lacan sees.

In Kleist's play, *Penthesilea*, Penthesilea is Queen of the Amazons. Alone among the women she leads, she has the privi-lege (and the tragic fate) of being able to know in advance who her sexual partner will be. The Amazons, who are sworn to virginity and hostility to the masculine sex, and have severed their left breast as a sign of their opposition, are warriors in an ironic cause: their aim, their imperative, is to bring prisoners — men — back alive from their battles for the exclusive purpose of mating with them, thereby regenerating their culture and their society. The sexual congress takes place during a festival of roses in which the men conquered by the sword are conquered again by the womanly arts of seduction. It also takes place in a sacred, hidden, closed-off locale: the Temple of Diana. None is sup-posed to have preferred one man to another before this event; only Penthesilea, whose mother has died too soon, had to have her destined sexual partner's identity revealed to her: Achilles the Greek.

Achilles is as perfect a specimen of 'manhood' as anyone could conceive: as perfect a model of his sex as Penthesilea is of hers (except of course for the one negative attribute, the missing breast). He is amorous, lusty, anxious to practise the art of heroic not seductive love, love as conquest alone. His pride is engaged by the hostility and attacks of Penthesilea, who fights him only because that is the means her culture commands she undertake in order to be an instrument of its reproduction.

But there is a problem. For Penthesilea is driven, furiously madly driven, towards Achilles, but without ever knowing exactly why. Oh, she knows conceptually what is to take place 'in the temple of Diana' — within the law. But she does not understand the reproductive act. She keeps trying to approximate what 'must happen' within the walls of the temple, staying to the agricultural imagery that has been her only direct experience of fecundation and growth of new life.

Her sheer ignorance is a source of major misapprehensions between her and Achilles. In a series of mock conquests and pseudo-yieldings, Achilles approaches the Queen with the intent of 'conquest' in his own manner: he will pretend she has conquered him so that he can 'have his pleasure with her'. The Queen, who has actually lost the battle, is relieved that she will be able to comply with the Law and be 'with' (somehow, she cannot quite picture how) this member of the opposite sex (who moves her strangely) in the only place she is allowed to be with a man — the temple of Diana. Achilles thinks very concretely only of the sexual pleasure he will have with her, and of his denial to his companions that he loves her. But he is as drawn to her as she to him. (He has allayed his fellow warriors' fears that he is 'soft' on Penthesilea by telling them that he will bring her home to Greece with him as his concubine — even wife, as long as she will give him 'a son'.)

Each bound to their culture's own way of subjecting the self to death by reproduction, but equally ignorant of the double face of sexuality, desire and love, the tragic outcome is already foreseen. But Penthesilea, as a form of Psyche, has been literally kept in the dark, and she bears the destructive force. Unable to penetrate the ambiguity, the veil that covers the genital act, Penthesilea's conscious mind collapses before the mystery. She analogises human sexual desire to the only desire she has ever known — purely verbal expressions of want, coupled with an imagery which is only animal in its model. In the final 'battle' —

in which Achilles, 'knowing' he is loved, also 'knows' that Penthesilea will never harm him since the object of the Amazon's conquest is the preservation and perpetuation of life — Penthesilea becomes literal with a vengeance. Taking her dogs with her she descends on the hapless, foolish and ill-armed Achilles and tears him limb from limb. When she regains her senses she kills herself over her deed, but not before she has 'explained' that the metaphors have all failed, they could not sustain the 'drive' for ever. How many times, she asks, has a lover told her man that she could 'just eat him up'?

Reframing the Ideology of Love beyond the Law

Kant claimed that to view anything from the point of view of an aim or an end (from the perspective of closure, that is) is to act ideologically.[7] The phenomenal manifestation, ideologically, of the 'end' towards which humans organise their sacrifice of immediate bodily and familial pleasure for union with a member of the opposed sex is the *child*, whose appearance and education restart the cycle.

One might suppose that by eschewing the 'end' of the cultural drive (reproduction), and its representative, the child, that one could be liberated from Oedipus and his imperatives. Once Freud has demystified the structure, why has it not 'withered away'?

Lacan gives us a better way of understanding the accelerating power of culture which persists above and beyond its provisional and ideological manifestations or formations which operate only at the *imaginary* level. The Symbolic Order as an Unconscious, rather than as a recognised, set of conventional values dominates the Imaginary: the 'concept' is the 'god' of the image, just as the transcendental signified is the god of the signifier. As such we are always waiting for the image to betray, reveal, manifest, this 'god', which depends on revelation and yet can never make an appearance as such. We 'know' it only ideologically, yet its drive is to be taken universally, as the one and only, the transcendent value.

Lacan's incessant fascination with the topic of love is, I think, an excellent illustration of the way he sought to examine the ideological powers exercised by culture to achieve not only its reproduction, but its universalisation as the only (unconscious) set of values.

Begin with 'romantic love' as one form — the imaginary form — of driving the individual to overcome bodily and familial associations by providing the aim of genital union. 'Civilised' love (non-incestuous love, love not directed solely towards the self) requires the construction of an *ideal* love alternative to narcissistic and familial *eros*. The ideological motivation for leaving auto-erotic and familial pleasures is generally termed 'love'. The construction of human out of animal desire, Hegel claimed, depended upon a moment of idealisation, which demanded the deferral of satisfaction in favour of its image: the promise of future enjoyment, joy.

As an idealisation, a first-order ideology, this romantic love undergoes a transformation: ideologies must act to cover contradictions in their imperatives by *anamorphising* their aims, that is, by occulting them from one perspective while leaving traces that can make their appearance inferable. If, for example, the waking imperative for sexual union is solely for procreation, then the dream will be of a love disengaged from commitment to a child. If the declared imperative is romantic love, the actual, though tacit, imperative may be to produce a child, etc.[8]

Such contradictions are, classically, the 'stuff' of human, cultural life. The question remains, 'how does a fairly simple ideology become a *drive*?' The love-ideology serves as example. A supplementary order appears when the values of a symbolic order become unconscious, that is, are merely 'conceptual' and presumed to be detached from — to stand over and above — their imaginary forms. Here 'love' is not simply a set of charming images, logically related so as to produce a desired end — the child, cultural surplus — but a promise — of something even more significant, more valuable.

If the aim of *sacrifice* is the *union of the sexes*, the *drive* within it is to specify its *concept as union or unity, oneness*. Love, from the standpoint of the symbolic order, is the imperative (the conceptualisation of this imaginary structure) simply to 'make one'. If the 'Law' of love is to produce a child, or to sacrifice one's individuality to the collective, the 'Law' of that 'Law' — its *concept* — comes forth as a universal commandment to to reduce two to one, multiplicity to unity.

Under this universalisation, all the aspects of cultural life, including lived experience, come under its hegemony, its singular value. We must 'make one' out of two separate beings (*the married couple*), 'make one' (in the form of a *child*), 'make one' out of all the potential meanings of a term, 'make one' out of all the diversity of human groups; one gender out of the several available models. *E pluribus unum*: one god, one people. From the symbolic point of view, the particulars and rich imagery associated with male and female, parent and child, ethnicity and politics must be sacrificed as, literally, indifferent; only the concept matters: *'faire un'*.[9]

Notes

1. Here my reading shows the affinity between Lacan and Derrida, particularly in Derrida's use of Lacan as a starting-point for breaking out of the impasses, the closed circles of the signifier and into another way of framing the sign. Lacan has uncovered the mark of metaphor, its omnipotence and omnipresence in culture. He has suggested its mark bars metonymy, or linkage through the process of splitting or separation. Derrida, while agreeing that the metonymic is the only counter to metaphor, radicalises more methodically the dissymmetry of metaphor and metonymy, the 'irreducibility' of metaphor, its primacy over the proper name. Like Rousseau, for whom the figure preceded the proper, Derrida undoes the fiction of the 'other scene' ruled by metonymy as a 'before'. My compromise is that we must detemporalise the positioning of the two scenes: neither should be a 'scène primitive' and the other only its 'repetition' — each is already there; the two are contemporary: it is a question of how we inhabit each scene. Methodologically, this amounts to accepting Derrida's *double séance*, the 'à la fois'. Perhaps this will prevent the signifier's indiscriminate operation of cutting off — an unworthy body part, a family member, a social scene.

2. In Lacan's writing, the scene that is dominated by the metaphoric mode is *culture* in the mode of an *economy*: it relegates the scene in which a metonymic mode holds sway to *dream*, ruling and regulating it even there. In dreams inserted into metaphorical culture-frames, metonymy — as displacement — works in the service of disconnection. In the dream, on the other hand, it is condensation, a 'metaphoric' process (Wilden, 1972: 47–50) that, through the mechanism of over-determination, allows associations which have been blocked (by constant displacement) to move through its formless form (that of a knot) as through a 'switchpoint' to make the connections. In the dream-scene, metaphor offers itself as free, in the guise of metaphor-as-

condensation it works to find resemblances. Its similarity mode dominates the selective, negating the side of metaphor. Displacement dream, on the other hand, is what does the work of disconnection, it is 'metonymy' without the function of forming a tie, a relationship. In the dream-scene, metonymy-as-displacement disconnects.

3. The aim of the transference is not, Lacan insists, the identification with the analyst (*4FC*, 271); instead it is a reading, a re-reading of the signifier, especially of the *petit a*, 'the object around which the drive moves' (257) by isolating the *a* 'at the greatest possible distance from the I that the subject calls on the analyst to embody' (273). The analyst, that is, has to fall from idealisation.

4. Sigmund Freud, *Dora: An Analysis of a Case of Hysteria* (N.Y., Collier, 1962).

5. See *Diacritics* (Spring 1983), esp. Neil Hertz, 'Dora's Secrets, Freud's Techniques', pp. 65–79.

6. Freud claims it was Dora who deprived him of the 'satisfaction of affording a far more radical cure for her troubles' (144), blaming the position of the women in the symbolic order for the lack of satisfaction the order itself commands. See Freud's inverse love-grammar related to paranoia, erotomania, etc., as contradictions of a single proposition 'I (a man) love him (a man)' (*SE*, XIII, 62–5).

7. Luc Ferry and Alain Renaut, 'D'un retour a Kant', *Ornicar?* 20–1 (1980), 191 ff., discuss Kant's analysis of the categories (especially of grammar) as leading to the ontological question; and of science as leading to metaphysics through a valorisation of absorption of the real by the conceptual. Science becomes ideological via a fetishistic procedure of speculating on its final achievement (195) in which the real would have become transparent to theory.

8. See Gayle Rubin, 'The Traffic in Women', in Rayna M. Reiter (ed.), *Towards an Anthropology of Women* (N.Y., Monthly Review Press, 1975), for a discussion of the ideology of reproduction and Marxism — one makes babies to supply the labour for industry. Rubin is critical of Marxist analyses. Although she 'counters' Marx and Engels' analyses of the family and the ideology of the family with Freud and Lacan, she is too (anthropologically) certain that culture is a universal fact of human life that cannot, at a fundamental level, be questioned for her to understand Lacan.

9. Here a literary example: In the James novel *What Maisie Knew* Maisie Farange becomes a kind of test case for the state of civilisation. Her parents, Beale and Ida Farange, have decided, since they are only ordinary when they are together, that 'they would be much more striking apart', and consequently dissolve their matrimonial union. The divorce divides the child between them, *à la* Solomon.

From a structural point of view Maisie, by mere virtue of her being a child, operates the cultural mechanism: she evokes what James in the Preface calls 'the moral sense' in this amoral setting, albeit never in her own parents. She even knows this is the positive side of her function when she perspicaciously asserts that it is she who has 'brought you two

175

together', referring to her stepmother and her stepfather. (She remains for some time unaware of the romance between the two for which her existence is a convenient 'cover'.) But her parents have clearly escaped the 'intent' of the Oedipal paradigm, at least in its ideological form of the patriarchal household. They negate the ideologies of marriage (fidelity) romantic love (their serial, loveless, liaisons) and parenthood (Maisie is rejected by both).

In every way these two are purely 'symbolic' people: they are known for their handsome appearance in public, and particularly for their clothes. They also live strictly according to their 'word': not the Oedipal promise, but the word they freely give themselves — each vows to make the other miserable. This vow (Lacan might have used the term *voeu*, with its ambiguous meaning both as wish and as vow) legislates their every action. It is the one thing they both stick to with unswerving fidelity. And they derive absolutely no happiness from it. They are bitter, unhappy people: the symbolic order, as distinct from the ideological order, never promises 'happiness', only freedom (and duty).

Their 'law' is a second-order law. If love is the idealisation and deferral of desire, and unity the universal concept of love, then the parents of Maisie are doing purely symbolic work, they labour for the concept. Singled out, these two have 'become one' in the most abject and literal sense of the term, two egos incapable of even an imaginary relationship to another being. Symbolic imagery aims at destroying all association between the self and the other.

This barrenness and nakedness of the symbolic order is also an ideological veil, however, since at the extreme point where it inverts the worn-out Oedipal ideology — turning erotic 'union' into sheer numerical one-ness, alone-ness, and into an inverse, 'immoral' order — it is still an ideology, an anamorphosis. The Symbolic Order continues to derive its force from a division that appears as a form of unity (the solidity of the ego). The liberated or 'free' egos of Beale and Ida are more enslaved, more bound to the symbolic drive towards atomisation, than they could ever have been to anything in the waning ideology, with its implicit demands for sacrifices: they sever connections with others quite willingly and without even the promise of happiness for the ceremonial 'cutting off'.

The ideological 'cover' is no longer the child: Maisie succeeds only briefly as an ideological child, the patriarchal ideological version of Oedipus is by the beginning of the twentieth century perhaps too shop-worn to clothe adequately the symbolic order. But James, like Lacan, lets us know that this purely symbolic law has its 'police', its concrete institution. As the novel demonstrates, one concrete form of value effectively fuels the drive: money, the barred subject, $. And its lack.

Index

177

Index

178

Index

Index

Index